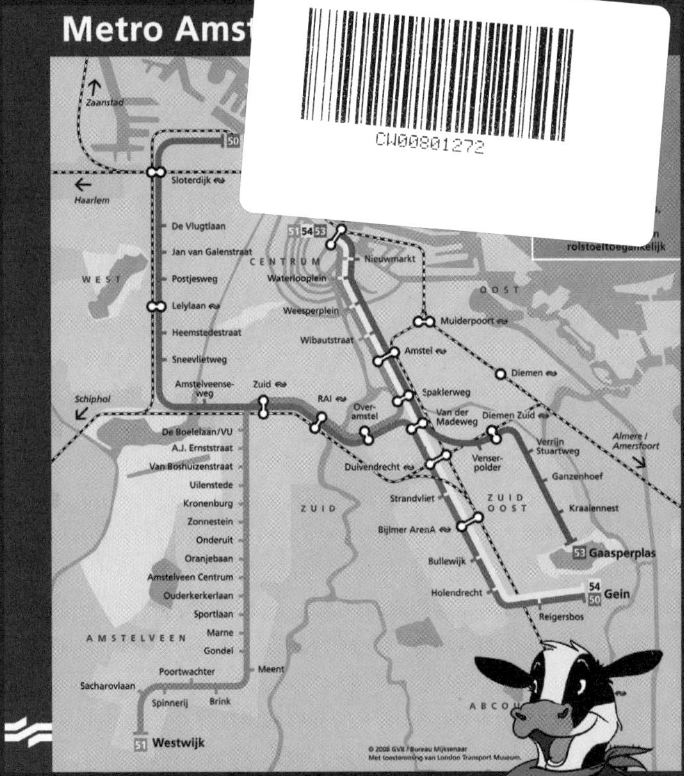

Metro Amst
Zaanstad
Haarlem
Schiphol
Almere / Amersfoort
50
51
53
54
Sloterdijk
De Vlugtlaan
Jan van Galenstraat
Postjesweg
Lelylaan
Heemstedestraat
Sneevlietweg
Amstelveenseweg
Zuid
RAI
Overamstel
Duivendrecht
De Boelelaan/VU
A.J. Ernststraat
Van Boshuizenstraat
Uilenstede
Kronenburg
Zonnestein
Onderuit
Oranjebaan
Amstelveen Centrum
Ouderkerkerlaan
Sportlaan
Marne
Gondel
Meent
Poortwachter
Sacharovlaan
Spinnerij
Brink
Westwijk
CENTRUM
WEST
OOST
ZUID
ZUID OOST
AMSTELVEEN
ABCOU
Nieuwmarkt
Waterlooplein
Weesperplein
Wibautstraat
Muiderpoort
Amstel
Diemen
Spaklerweg
Van der Madeweg
Diemen Zuid
Verrijn Stuartweg
Ganzenhoef
Kraaiennest
Gaasperplas
Venserpolder
Strandvliet
Bijlmer ArenA
Bullewijk
Holendrecht
Reigersbos
Gein
rolstoeltoegankelijk
© 2008 GVB / Bureau Mijksenaar
Met toestemming van London Transport Museum.

Vaarroutes, haltes en overstapmogelijkheden
Gvb FERRiES
NDSM-TERREIN
Houthavenveer
Houthaven
Distelwegveer
DISTELWEG
Het IJ
TASMANSTR.
VAN DIEMEN STRAAT
HOUTMANKADE
NDSM-werfveer
Westerdok
BUIKSLOTERWEG
Buiksloterwegveer
MEEUWEN LAAN
IJPLEIN
Ijpleinveer
DE RUYTERKADE
Centraal Station
stads-, streekvervoer, NS
SUMATRAKADE

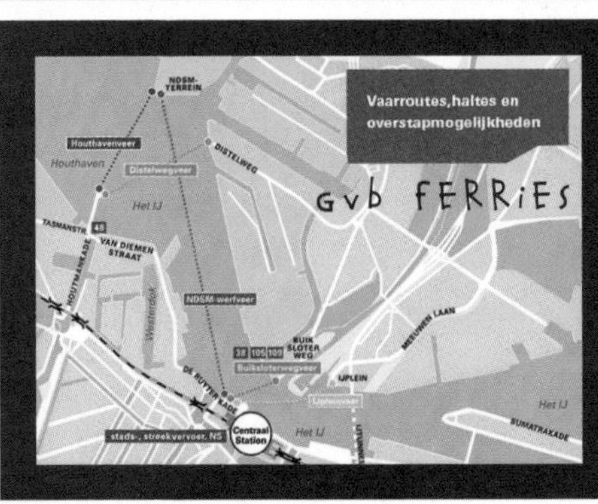

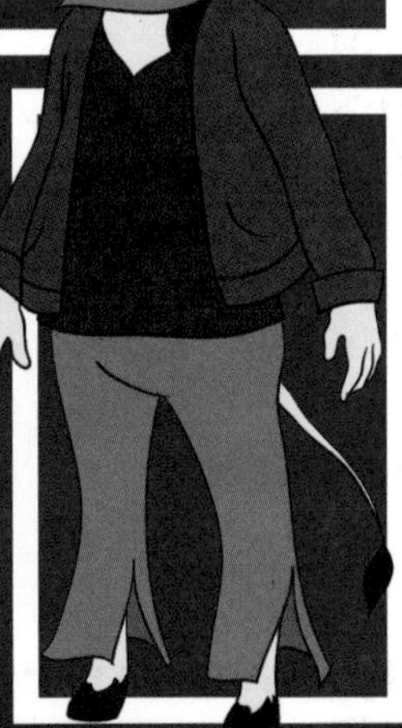

JUNIOR JETSETTERS™

guide to

Junior Jetsetters™ Guide to Amsterdam
First edition February 2009
ISBN-13: 978-0-9784601-2-9

Published in Toronto by Junior Jetsetters Inc.
3044 Bloor St. W., Suite 550, Toronto, ON M8X 2Y8 (Canada)
Text: Pedro F. Marcelino, Slawko Waschuk
Sub-Editor: Anna Humphrey
Characters: Kim Sokol
Illustrations: Maurice Van Tilburg (www.atelieropen.nl)
Cover Design: Pedro F. Marcelino, set in Casual Font by A.J. Palmer
Cover Art: Maurice Van Tilburg, Tapan Gandhi (logo), Kim Sokol (stamp).

Special Thanks to: Tommy Grießler, Romi Stahl, Arnild Van de Velde, Edith Brouwer, Maurice Van Tilburg, Daiana Vasquez, Fefa Guimarães, Pedro Cézar Mendes, Sheridan College Institute of Technology.

Library and Archives Canada Cataloguing in Publication

Marcelino, Pedro F., 1978-
Junior Jetsetters guide to Amsterdam / Pedro F. Marcelino, Slawko Waschuk ; edited by Anna Humphrey ; illustrated by Kim Sokol, Maurice van Tilburg and Tapan Gandhi.

ISBN 978-0-9784601-2-9

1. Amsterdam (Netherlands)--Guidebooks--Juvenile literature. I. Waschuk, Slawko, 1974- II. Humphrey, Anna, 1979- III. Sokol, Kim, 1987- IV. Tilburg, Maurice van, 1971- V. Gandhi, Tapan, 1986- VI. Title. VII. Title: Guide to Amsterdam.

DJ411.A53M37 2009   j914.92'3520473   C2008-907874-8

Printed and bound in China by Everbest Printing Co Ltd.

your list of stuff to see and do

top 5 things to do in amsterdam

amsterdam attractions

activities in amsterdam

out-of-town and further afield

your list of stuff to see and do

what do you know about amsterdam and the netherlands?

Amsterdam is the capital, and largest city, of the Netherlands. Some of its trademarks are the windmills scattered all over the city, and the battered bikes you'll see everywhere. In fact, Amsterdam is often called the bike capital of the world! The city is also famous for its canals, which are a bit like the ones in Venice.

Amsterdam was once a bunch of islands, becoming a city only once dams were built and watery areas filled in to create land for houses. These landfills are called *polders*, and some regions in the Netherlands stand on soil that was 'invented' by the Dutch. In Amsterdam, water makes up a quarter of the total area of the city, and there are about 1,500 bridges over the 10 km of canals, resulting in over 90 islands (not to mention the river IJ and the IJssel Lake.

how cool is that?

Of course, all this earned Amsterdam a few nicknames, such as 'Venice of the North', or Mokum (a Yiddish word for 'place' or 'safe haven'). Young Amsterdammers write down A'dam to economize! They also call the Netherlands 'our little (cold) frogland', no one really knows why. Perhaps it describes seriously horrible clouds and damp cold.

But, Amsterdam's fast-changing weather also made it the perfect home for some of the world's most famous artists, like Rembrandt and Vincent van Gogh, who got their inspiration in its golden light filtered through some nasty clouds! Don't worry, there is plenty of sun around, at least in the summer time! Make sure you enjoy it.

a little history

it wasn't a great spot for a city

More than 1,000 years ago, the area where Amsterdam now stands was a collection of small islands and marshlands. It didn't exactly seem like a great spot to build a city, but small farming settlements existed here and there. One was set up around a small dam on the Amstel River and was called Aemstelledamme ('dam on the Amstel').

...but they built one anyway!

This small community eventually became a city around 1300, and experienced a boost in the 14th and 15th centuries. The areas around the dam were filled in to create land for houses and other buildings, only a few of which (such as the Oude Kerk and Nieuwe Kerk) survive today. Buldings were mostly made of wood back then, and they didn't survive until today. Amsterdam's oldest house, Het Houten Huis, is an exception. When large fires destroyed three quarters of the city in 1451 and 1452, every house finally started to be built out of of stone. Smart move!

there was war for 80 years

Around this time, trading agreements were established with an alliance of cities in the Baltic Sea — the Hanseatic League. This helped Amsterdam become the most important city in the Netherlands. But the sudden wealth also made it a covetted trophy. The Spanish King eventually took over the Netherlands (or Lower Countries, as it was then known), and ruled it from the

the distance, and paying very little attention to the wishes of Dutch people. Finally, in the 16th century there was a rebellion against King Philip II of Spain, who was then the ruler. The Dutch were fed up with new taxes and with being harassed about religion by the Spanish Inquisition.

This rebellion led to the Eighty Years' War, which in turn led to Dutch independence. As religious intolerance was increasing all over Europe, many people came to Amsterdam to find a safe place to live, where they could practise their own religions in peace. The largest groups were Jews from Spain and Portugal and Huguenots from France. Over time, these events helped make the Netherlands one of the most tolerant and receptive countries with respect to religion.

the golden age began

During the Golden Age (1585-1672), trade with other countries was at an all-time high. Amsterdam became one of the richest cities in the world, overseeing ships sailing to North America, Indonesia, Brazil and Africa. The city's location made it the perfect spot for shipping stuff to and from other European cities, and Amsterdam quickly became the financial centre of Europe. Many lands were claimed overseas, and would later become Dutch colonies. The largest company involved in trading was the Dutch East India Company, a powerful merchant organization which operated much like a multinational does today.

The Golden Age also helped to shape the city. Many historic buildings were constructed then, including the town hall (now the Royal Palace), Westerkerk and lots of houses around the canals. Art was also in, and Dutch masters like Rembrandt were the envy of Europe.

The Plague Plagued the People

As a busy port, Amsterdam benefited from a lot of good fortune, but it was also vulnerable to infections brought over from other countries. Near the end of the Golden Age, the bubonic plague — or Black Death — arrived big time. This terrible disease had already freaked out half of Europe, and the terrible outbreaks in Amsterdam killed over 10 percent of the population!

The Dutch Republic Under Siege

Between 1672 and 1795, the Dutch weren't the only ones with ships that were exploring and trading around the world. Spain had been a naval power for a while, and Portugal was an old enemy of the Dutch, whose navy, as well as its fierce pirates and corsairs, often raided Portuguese colonies like Brazil.

The English and French, on the other hand, attacked the Dutch Republic in 1672, when political disputes heightened, but the Netherlands survived the attack. William III of Orange, with the help of Austria, Spain and Prussia was able not only to repel the invading French, but even to invade England in return. He was proclaimed king and his wife, Mary Stuart, queen. Through all the turmoil, Amsterdam continued powerful as before, expanding by the day.

Then They Got Attacked Again

During the French Revolution, Napoléon Bonaparte of France invaded the country and started a monarchy, with his brother Louis Napoléon as King. The capital was shifted from The Hague to Amsterdam at that time, and the city hall on the Dam Square became the King's residence. Within a few years, the Netherlands became part of the French Empire, with Napoléon Bonaparte as the Emperor. The economy suffered, of course, and the lack of care by the usurper caused much of the city to fall into great disrepair. England, a sworn enemy of France during this revolutionary period, blockaded the continent with its powerful navy, and took over Dutch colonies one by one.

Things were looking up, then down, then up, then down again

In 1813, Napoléon Bonaparte was finally defeated. Even though Amsterdam's trade recovered, it never reached the heights of the Golden Age again. William VI of Orange was crowned King William I of the United Kingdom of the Netherlands, while, with the help of the French, the southern provinces formed the independent Kingdom of Belgium. The government of the Netherlands stayed in The Hague, where it had been during the union. Over time, Amsterdam developed, first with the arrival of the railways, then the commerce of diamonds and lots of people with a lot of energy arriving to the city (and doubling its population).

At the start of the 20th century, World War I affected most of Europe, but the Netherlands remained neutral. The war did affect the city in many ways, though, because naval blockades put a stop to almost all trade with the East Indies. After the war, Amsterdam managed to get its economy back on track. But in 1929 a huge economic crisis (the depression) hit the world. It was around that time, and partly to provide some jobs, that the Zuiderzee (a shallow inlet) was separated from the North Sea by the Afsluitdijk (a dike that created the IJsselmeer). Amsterdam lost its direct access to the sea, precisely the reason of its past success.

things got really, really bad.

During World War II, the Netherlands tried to remain neutral again, but this time it wasn't so easy. German troops invaded the country in May 1940. Queen Wilhemina went into exile in London and Ottawa with her children. The war devastated Amsterdam, and most of the Jews were deported to concentration camps, while many Dutch men were sent to work in Germany. Supplies were non-existent and many people died from the cold and from hunger. In the final days of World War II, the city was finally liberated by Canadian troops. After the war, Amsterdam was re-built better than ever. Many of the buildings that had been destroyed or were unkept were demolished to make room for new ones, respecting the medieval street plan and sometimes recreating the look of the old buildings that were there before.

amsterdam today

Amsterdam survived all this, and today is known as a free, open and tolerant city. Dutch people believe that everyone should be allowed to be and act however they choose, as long as they don't interfere with other people's lives. Personal expression can be seen all over, from the way people dress to the way they enjoy their time, so be sure to keep an open mind... A'dam is one of the most exciting, unique and cute cities ever!

get ready for your trip!

Visit the Amsterdam Tourism & Convention Board site (www.iamsterdam.com), for more information you may need during your visit to this watery city, and some insider advice! If you have any tips or questions for Junior Jetsetters, email us at: **FEEDBACK@JUNIORJETSETTERS.CA.**

Mies de Mouflon
Sandrijn de Swan
Beeuw de Boar

Jordi

daan dE dutch SHEPHERd
HENK dE HERON
KEiRa
Roos dE FRisian cow

it's not the flying dutchman but still a splendid old ship!

The Dutch East India Company was started in 1602 to increase trade and maintain close relations with Dutch colonies in Asia, notably Batavia (which is nowadays part of Indonesia). The company had a huge fleet of ships for travelling back and forth. A big ship called the Amsterdam was built in 1748 to transport items between the Dutch Republic and the Far East. Like her sister ships, on the outbound journey, the ship would typically carry 300 men, as well as bricks, wool, wine and silver. On the way back, it would carry purchased goods, like spices, tea, fabrics and porcelain from Asia… and only the 100-or-so men who didn't die on the way, or stay in the colonies. Almost all of these men lived in the lower deck, with their horses, livestock, cheese and rats. Sailors would often hide cheese in their socks for a snack. It was really tight, steamy and a real mess.

In 1749, the Amsterdam set sail for the first time from the Frisian island of Texel (see page 126). During a storm, the rudder snapped and the ship was beached off the coast of England. Before long, it sank in the mud, and would never be freed. All of the crew survived. The hull of the ship is still there and can sometimes be seen during low tide.

Between 1985 and 1990, about 400 volunteers built a replica of the Amsterdam, using tools that were available when the original ship was built. The ship is now moored next to Science Center NEMO (see page 18) while its home dock at the national Maritime Museum (Scheepvaartmuseum), just across the canal, is being renovated.

Eastindiaman 'Amsterdam' (Maritime Museum)

Het VOC-schip Amsterdam (Nederlands Scheepvaartmuseum)

JUNIOR TOP 5 JETSETTERS

cool, yeah?

The Eastindiaman ships sailed a total of 4,800 times while the company lasted.

Even large wooden boats like the Amsterdam have leaks. Pumping water permanently is necessary at all times to keep it afloat!

walk Right through a painting

Rembrandtplein is a square in Amsterdam named after Rembrandt Harmenszoon van Rijn, (a.k.a. the painter, Rembrandt). Rembrandt was one of the most important Dutch masters during the Golden Age. He was well known for his portraits, self-portraits, etches and scenes from the Bible. His most famous work is *The Night Watch* (*De Nachtwacht* in Dutch), which is on display in the Rijksmuseum (see page 64). The huge painting portrays a group (or company) moving out, led by Captain Frans Banning Cocq and his lieutenant, Willem van Ruytenburch. Captain Cocq is the one with the red sash. Although there are many people in the painting, three stand out: the Captain, the lieutenant and a small girl.

The Night Watch has been recreated in a 3-D version to celebrate the 400th anniversary of Rembrand's birth. Twenty-two of the characters, made of bronze, have been placed in front of a statue of Rembrandt, in the centre of the Rembrandplein, where the master can 'watch' his work. You'll feel like you're walking through a painting! You can touch the statues, hug them, pose with them and feel like you're actually in the Golden Ages! The square is also a very popular local hangout surrounded by cafés, terraces, diamond factories, canals and souvenir shops!

cool, yeah?

Legally, Rembrandt's first name was spelled Rembrant. For some reason, known only to him, he added the 'd' when he was in his 20s.

The Night Watch is actually called Company of Frans Banning Cocq and Willem van Ruytenburch.

Rembrandt Square + 3d Night Watch

Rembrandtplein en Nachtwacht in 3D

24 JUN 10
11:01:02
inframetrics
IMAGE X1
10.5
34.7
-40°C
90°C
THERMACAM
ε=1.00 R1

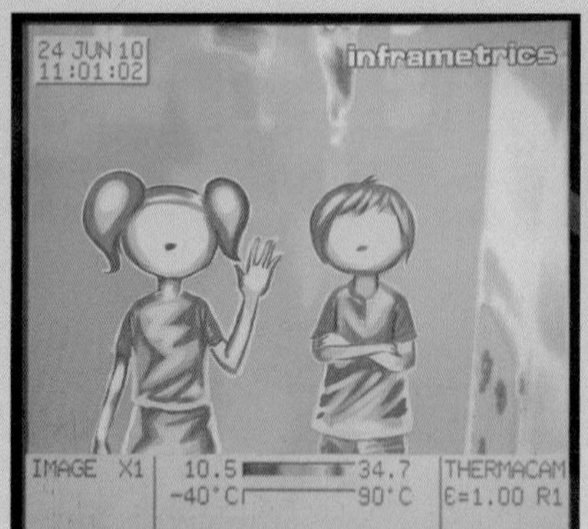

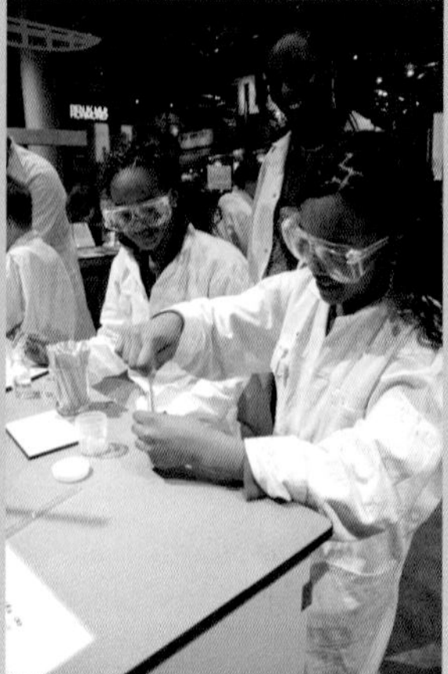

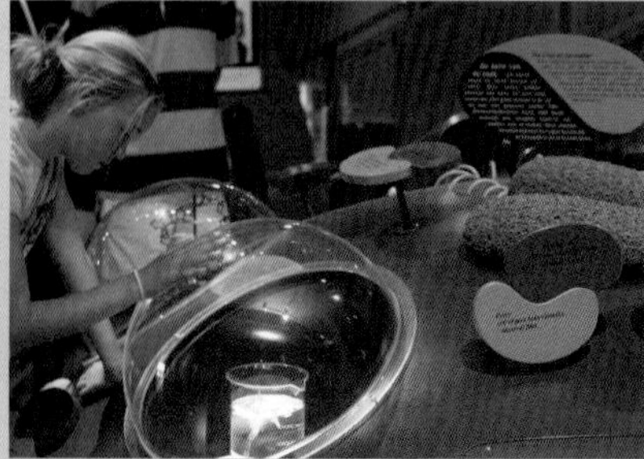

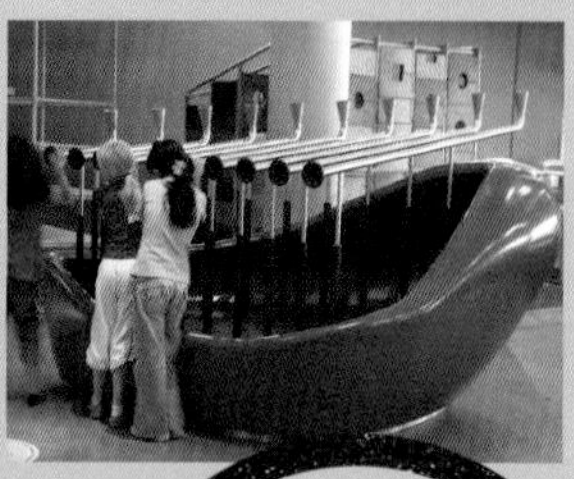

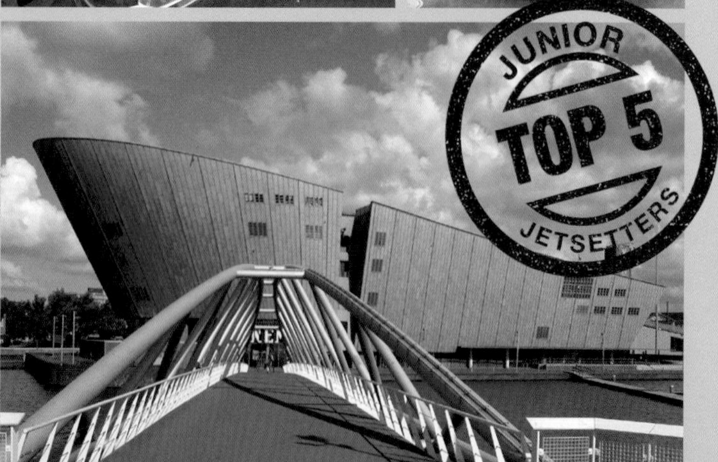

JUNIOR
TOP 5
JETSETTERS

you must touch everything

Adenine, cytosine, guanine and thymine. Not sure what they are? They're possibly the four most important bases ever discovered. They're also what make up DNA, or deoxyribonucleic acid. DNA carries the genetic information needed for all living organisms to develop and work properly. That includes the tiniest of flowers, the slimiest of slugs, the biggest of bears and even us humans. Anything that is alive has DNA. Of course, DNA today is used for many things. Scientists use it to learn about diseases and how to treat them, and police use it to figure out who committed crimes. There's so much to learn about DNA and the Science Center NEMO is the place to start.

But Codename: DNA is just one section of this huge science centre. There's so much to do in this boat shaped building! Other exhibits demonstrate cause and effect and action and reaction, why the world works the way it does, amazing buildings and bridges, electricity, the brain, new fuel technology, water and computers and information technology. The hands-on chemistry lab is open to all. Stop by and try conducting your own experiments. (And in the summer, go up to the rooftop deck to sunbathe and take in the best view in Amsterdam!)

cool, yeah?

An Italian architect called Renzo Piano designed the boat-shaped NEMO.

NEMO means 'nobody'. They called it that because visitors feel like they're in no man's land, where fantasies seem to become real.

TRAVEL AROUND THE TROPICS AND BACK IN JUST A FEW HOURS

In the Golden Age, the Netherlands was the leader in world trade. The might of the Dutch merchant and military fleet outdid that of other great European powers of the time: Portugal, Spain and England. Dutch merchants and explorers travelled the world, starting colonies in Africa, Asia, the Caribbean and North and South America.

For a long time, the Tropenmuseum (Museum of the Tropics) has been displaying all things related to the Dutch colonies—mostly Indonesia. After Indonesian independence in 1949, the museum started to focus also on all the other 'tropics'—the Middle East, Africa and Latin America. The museum's collection is one of the greatest in Europe, and it's a completely interactive experience that's geared toward kids like you. You'll learn how everything in Amsterdam came to be, and its tight connections to world history.

Centuries of tropical exchanges made Dutch society really multicultural. Other countries, like Indonesia, Suriname and some islands in the Caribbean also maintain bits of Dutch heritage!

At the museum you'll learn more about how, back in the Golden Age, the Dutch East India Company had control of all colonial activities east of Africa and off the coast of Chile. The Dutch West India Company was later set up to control the parts of the world that weren't already controlled by the other company, but both of these multinationals competed with foreign companies.

The Tropenmuseum Junior is a special section of the museum especially for children aged 6 to 12 (parents aren't even allowed in!). It brings foreign, non-western cultures to life through hands-on exhibits and activities. One season the museum might be transformed into a labyrinth of Mumbai life, the next season it could throw you right back to life in the Forbidden City in Beijing. From a daily commute in a Mumbai train to the smells in the alleyways of an Egyptian market, and from the sounds of an African village to the bustle of a tropical metropolis, everything makes you feel like you've travelled halfway across the world. You'll be surprised to see your parents waiting for you back in the Netherlands, just outside the door!

vivid colourful paintings from an acclaimed artist

Van Gogh is one of the world's most famous artists, but he didn't begin his career until late in his life. His first job, as art dealer in The Hague, took him first to London and several years later to Paris where he grew interested in religion. When he was fired from his job, he decided to move to Amsterdam to study theology, but this didn't last long. He dropped out and became a preacher in a poor mining area in Belgium. It was here that he started to do charcoal sketches. Taking advice from his dear brother, Theo, he took up painting as a career, starting with painting lessons—something that would influence his later works. He also spent time in the Netherlands, Belgium and France. But van Gogh suffered from a serious mental illness, which eventually led him to cut off his own ear and later to commit suicide. And here's something else sad! Van Gogh only sold one painting while he was still alive! Nowadays, his works sell at auctions for millions a piece! The Van Gogh Museum features a large collection of his works. His landscapes, self-portraits and still-lifes are famous for their strong, bright colours, powerful brush strokes and patches of paint. Get a kids' audio tour at the front desk and follow the butterflies around the museum!

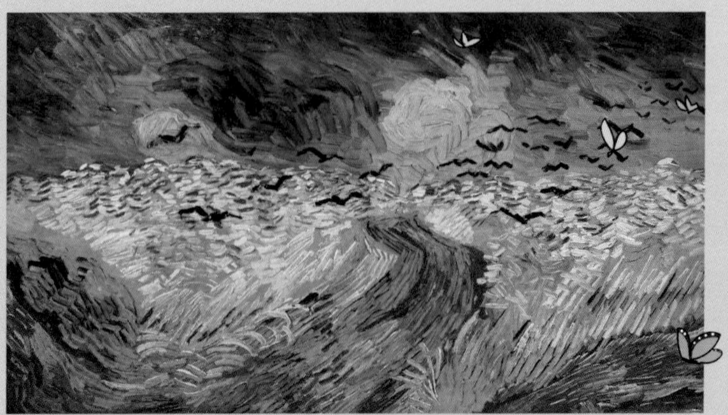

cool, yEaH?

His art career lasted only the last 10 years of his life, but those were jam-packed. All in all, he created about 2,000 works (900 paintings and 1,100 drawings). That's about 200 pieces per year — that is roughly one every two days!

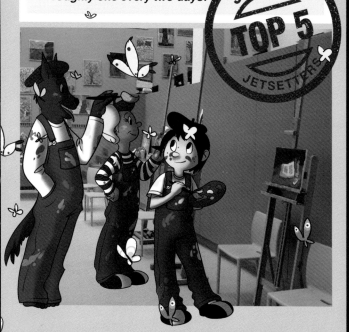

calling all football fans!!!

Like most Europeans, the Dutch are huge football (soccer) fans. They're crazy about the AFC Ajax (Amsterdamsche Football Club Ajax), Amsterdam's professional football club, and one of the three leading clubs in the country, together with PSV Eindhoven and Feyenoord. These three teams provide most of the players for the famous Dutch Orange or Mechanical Orange, the feared national side that is an eternal contender in European and world competitions alike.

Like cheering for any team, supporting Ajax is an emotional rollercoaster. The team has had some rocky years, and some amazing ones. Ajax has won the European Cup, The Treble (three important European cups in one season) and the Intercontinental Cup. In fact, other than Ajax, only two other clubs have won all three major European cups before (Bayern Munich, from Germany, and Juventus, from Italy).

Ajax, which has been a professional club since 1955, nowadays plays in the Amsterdam ArenA, opened since 1996. This arena has a retractable roof, and has been used as a model for a lot of other European stadiums. The stadium also has a great museum that tells the stories of the Ajax Football Club and of the Amsterdam ArenA. There are guided tours available, which will take you through the whole facility, including the press room, the control room and even the highest seats in the stadium. When it's not being used for football, many concerts are held in the stadium. It is pretty awesome to be inside!

cool, yeah?

The team's logo is a portrait of Ajax, a mythological Greek hero. The logo is drawn using 11 simple lines—one for each of the 11 players on a football team.

lEaRN to spEll youR NaME... iN EGyptiaN HiERoGlyphics!

When you think of archæology, you probably picture Ancient Egyptian mummies. The Ancient Egyptians' belief in the afterlife was what caused them to build the world's most recognizable monuments—the pyramids. Inside the pyramids, pharaohs were buried with all the possessions they would need in the afterlife. One thing they were buried with that you almost never hear about is the *ushabti* (sometimes called *ushapti*). Ushabtis are small figurines that were placed in the tombs as 'substitutes' for the dead person. This was important in case the person was called upon to do manual labour in the afterlife. The ushabtis would act as the deceased's servant-labourers. Some pharaohs had hundreds of them in their tombs, just in case... Talk about laziness!

cool, yEaH?

The museum's attic is packed with plaster casts of famous Roman and Greek statues (only open on special occasions).

Ancient Greek statues were not 'classic' white as they appear today, but were once painted in bright colours, signifying wealth and importance!

Like many museums of its kind, the Allard Pierson Museum has a large Egyptology section full of mummies and their stuff... But even though that's a cool part of history, Egypt isn't the only place with ancient artifacts!

The museum also has its share of artifacts from elsewhere in the ancient world: the Near East, Greece, Italy and Sicily, Etruria, Cyprus and Rome. They've even got a special computer. Type in your name and it will spell it out for you in hieroglyphics! How cool is that?

cool, yeah?

Boys and girls were separated in the orphanage. The museum corridor used to be an alleyway between the two wings. A bridge connects them now.

Kalverstraat, the street on which the museum stands, is the most expensive street on the Dutch Monopoly!

a glimpse of the golden age

Amsterdam's Golden Age. The city was growing. Business was booming. Amsterdam became Europe's financial centre. This was the period when the cityscape developed and the characteristic 'Amsterdam look' was born. It was then that the Royal Palace was built, although it was originally just the town hall. It was placed at the end of one of the major canals, which eventually was land filled to build the Damrak. At this time, Amsterdam took over Lisbon, Portugal, and Seville, Spain, as the wealthiest city in Europe. Ships sailed from here to destinations in the Americas, Indonesia, Brazil and Africa. You're about to re-live it all!

The main focus of the Amsterdam Historical Museum is life in the Golden Age and its naval heroes, although some models, objects and other items on display show how the city grew from a small settlement to a really powerful port. The museum is housed in buildings that were once the Civic Orphanage of Amsterdam. Some of the largest and most famous paintings of the Golden Age are shown between its two old wings, in the corridor that is part of the museum. Once you're done looking around, take the exit to the Begijnhof next door. Only women are allowed to live in this square, and it has been this way for centuries, and it has been perfectly preserved!

discover anne frank's life

It was the year 1942. Persecution of Jews by the Germans had increased to an intolerable level. A young Jewish girl called Anne Frank received a blank notebook for her 13th birthday. She immediately started using it as a diary. Less than a month later, her family and a few friends were forced into hiding in an Amsterdam attic to avoid arrest by the occupying Germans.

For the next two years, Anne recorded what life was like living in the 'Secret Annex'. The space was tight, dark and damp, and during the day they had to remain perfectly still, so as not to be heard downstairs and discovered by the Nazis. Eventually, Gestapo (the German Security Police) was tipped off, and the family was arrested and put on a train bound for Auschwitz concentration camp. Anne and her sister got sent to Bergen-Belsen—a concentration camp in Germany, where she died during a typhus epidemic.

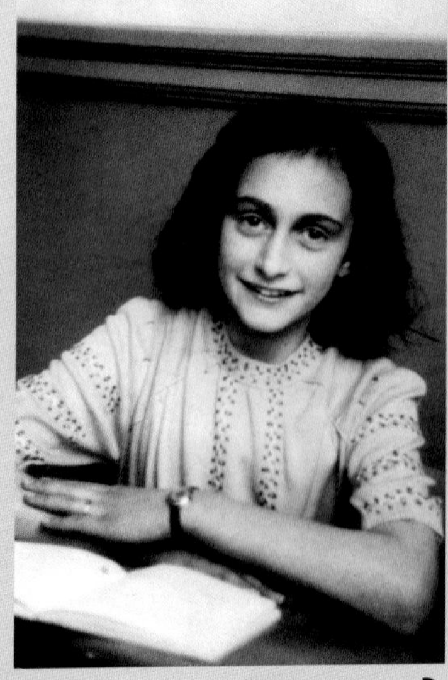

Anne Frank's diary was first published as a book in 1947, and was soon translated into over 50 languages. The book is known as *Anne Frank: The Diary of a Young Girl*, or *Anne Frank's Diary*. The house where the family hid is now a museum. It's one of the most touching monuments to one of the darkest moments of Jewish life in the city of Amsterdam, and will help you understand what life was like for Jewish people during the war, in the Netherlands and all over Europe.

cool, yeah?

Despite its sad real story, Anne Frank's Diary is one of the most popular books in the world, and people of all ages have read it and been touched by it. You can get a copy in almost any language at the Anne Frank House's store.

Only Anne's father, Otto Frank, survived the war. Upon his return to Amsterdam, he was given the diary by one of his former employees.

Step inside a canalside manor

Space in Amsterdam is a luxury, which explains why most original houses were built so narrow. They had steep staircases that were sometimes almost impossible to climb. (A thick rope running vertically in the building often served as a rail to help people go up without falling.) But there were wealthy merchants and people who were able to build houses that were much larger. Two of these are the **Museum Van Loon** and the **Museum Willet-Holthuysen**.

The **Van Loons** have been a prominent Dutch family since at least the Middle Ages. Several members of the family were the mayors of cities (including Amsterdam), and one was co-founder of the Dutch East India Company. Hendrick van Loon bought the house for his son, Willem, who was married to Queen Wilhelmina's Dame du Palais (lady-in-waiting). The house had many prominent guests while she lived there (until 1945). In that year it was restored and part of it was opened to the public. In addition to the house, there's a large garden and, farther back, a coach house that is now a private residence. The Van Loon family still owns the house, but they no longer live there. This museum is a chance to see an authentic noble Amsterdam canal house. Much of the art belongs to the Van Loon family, and dates back over the past few centuries.

The **Museum Willet-Holthuysen** is another fully-furnished canal house that is open to the public as a museum. The house was originally built for a mayor of Amsterdam. In 1895, the last owner, Mrs. Willet-Holthuysen, left the house to the city with the condition that it become a museum. Some of the rooms remain unchanged, while others have been restored to their original style. Here's another chance to take a look inside the typical life of a rich Dutch family.

cool, yeah?

The Van Loon family is still friends with the Dutch Royal Family. When Junior Jetsetters visited, the Queen had been over for dinner one week earlier

The Museum Willet-Holthuysen has a big collection of silverware, plates and books from the Golden Age as well as a large collection of art.

WHERE EVERYONE COMES AND EVERYONE GOES EVERYWHERE

You almost can't go to Amsterdam without seeing Centraal Station! That's because it's the main station in the city where trams, trains, buses, subways and even ferries all converge. You'll find it at the northern end of the Damrak, on the south bank of the IJ. City officials originally planned for the station to be in a different location, but government officials in The Hague believed a spot on the IJ would be better. This was controversial as it would create a city without a waterfront

cool, yeah?

Centraal Station was designed by the architects P.J.H. Cuypers and A.L. Van Gendt, and not by engineers, as was usual at that time.

instead of a city built around the river. The station was built on three man-made islands, supported by thousands of wooden poles. While in Amsterdam, you should at least try the yellow double-decker trains once. There are tons to choose from. Behind the station you can also catch a GVB ferry and cross the IJ for free to the little-known Amsterdam-Noord (SEE PAGE 92). But, even if you don't do any of those things, just hang out in the station and feel the pulse of the city for a while, watching people come and go! You'd think half of Amsterdam is always there!

amsterdam's 'living room'

Around the year 1270, people started building houses on both sides of the Amstel River. To connect the settlements and to protect them from the Zuiderzee (a large, shallow inlet of the North Sea) a dam was built. Over the years, this dam was made larger until it was big enough for a town square. The original settlements expanded, then combined to form a town. Soon ships started to moor at the dam, where sailors could load and unload goods. The square, which was first a fish market and then a general market, became the centre for business. And, before long, the town hall was built there.

cool, yeah?

The city got its name from this square's name: 'Amstel's dam'.

In the old days, Dutch market squares usually had a weigh house. Dam Square's weigh house was demolished by King Louis Bonaparte because it obstructed his view!!!

It then got converted to a Royal Palace by Louis Bonaparte, King of Holland and brother France's Emperor Napoléon I. Today, it is no longer home to the Royal family, but it's still available to them for official receptions. Keep your eyes open for a flag flying in the tower (that means a member of the royal family is inside). These days, the square is Amsterdam's 'living room'—a hub of activity with restaurants, shops, hotels, Madame Tussauds wax museum (SEE PAGE 48), the Nieuwe Kerk (SEE PAGE 52), and hundreds of bikes, rickshaws, trams and tourists. Summers are particularly lively, with mimes, street performers, musicians and sometimes even carnivals! It is the heart of Amsterdam.

at the heart of amsterdam

Your train pulls into Amsterdam Centraal Station. You gather your luggage and Junior Jetsetters guidebook. You make your way through the station until you reach the main doors. As you step outside, you see some really fancy buildings, including St. Nicolaaskerk. You're standing on the main street on your way to the main square. You're on the Damrak, at the heart of Amsterdam. The Damrak connects Centraal Station (SEE PAGE 34) to Dam Square (SEE PAGE 36) and goes onward to Rokin Street and the main canals.

At one time, the street was lined with the stock exchange and related financial institutions. 'Damrak' even became the term commonly used for the Amsterdam Stock Exchange (just as 'Wall Street' is used for the New York Stock Exchange). It's a popular shopping street (including De Bijenkorf, a famous department store)with restaurants, museums, trams and bicycles as far as you can see. If you're looking for Dutch wooden clogs to take home as a souvenir, here they are. But here's a tip: the farther down the Damrak and Rokin you walk, the cheaper your souvenirs will be!

cool, yeah?

The Damrak got its name from the 'rak' (or stretch of land) where it used to be, right by the Amstel's Dam.

cool, yEaH?

Diamonds (and other gems) are measured using carats. A carat is 200 mg. A diamond's price is based not only on how many carats it's got, but also on its purity and type of cut. The 121 Gassan's is a uniquely expensive diamond due to that cut. Currently, the largest polished diamond is The Golden Jubilee, weighing a whole 545.67 carats (109.13 g).

Prepare to be dazzled by really hard shiny carbon

In the 16th century, when no one else was interested in it, Sephardic Jews introduced a new industry to Amsterdam—diamond cutting. The city soon became a major diamond centre. In the 1870s, three brothers by the name of Boas set up a diamond factory. One brother ran the factory, while the other two bought raw stones in London and sold the polished and refined diamonds in Paris. Business was good… very good, actually! In just a few years, they had to build a new factory. Their business continued to grow until the Great Depression, when many workers moved to Antwerp in Belgium (the most important diamond centre in the world). During World War II, the Germans took over the building and tried to keep the factory running. Eventually, though, it was closed down and the Boas family members either moved out of the Netherlands or died in concentration camps.

In 1989, the factory was revived when Samuel Gassan bought it from the Boas family. Today, Gassan Diamonds carries on the diamond tradition. The company offers you the opportunity to see how rough diamonds are mined, then cut and polished into glittering and glamorous gems. You can even buy yourself one, if you've got the cash on you, that is! There are diamonds for all kinds of really high budgets...!

cool, yEaH?

The State Hermitage Museum and Hermitage Amsterdam are both near rivers. From a distance, they look really alike, and so do the cities themselves!

And it's not surprising that they look alike, either. Peter the Great designed Saint Petersburg after his travel to Amsterdam, and both cities are known as 'Venice of the North'.

a Russian museum in a'dam

When Peter the Great, Tsar of Russia, visited the Netherlands, he was captivated by Dutch art and began to buy paintings for his palaces back home. Catherine the Great, who became Tsaritsa years later, continued this interest when she picked up 200 paintings in Berlin. This was the start of the Hermitage Museum's collection in Saint Petersburg. Over her lifetime, Catherine bought tens of thousands of pieces, ranging from paintings and drawings to furniture, precious stones and silver, which were kept in the Winter Palace in Saint Petersburg, home to the Tsar. Her successors continued this tradition of collecting art, and new buildings were added gradually to hold the growing collection. In 1917, after the Russian Revolution, the state took control of the old imperial palaces and the waterfront complex became known as the State Hermitage Museum. It's one of the biggest museums in the world.

Over the last few years, the Hermitage has set up a few smaller museums to display its huge collection of art in different places. One of these museums is in Amsterdam. A historic building known as Amstelhof had just become available and was chosen as the location of the museum. The museum now displays temporary exhibitions in one building (the Neerlandia, a former nursing home) while the others are being renovated. Once completed, it will be one of the largest museums in Amsterdam, and one of the wings will be *just for kids*!

learn the origins of the leafy business of medicine

Between 1634 and 1637 thousands of people in the Dutch cities of Leiden and Utrecht died from the Black Death. Because of it, Amsterdam officials established Hortus Medicus—a herb garden with medicinal plants. The collection grew quickly in the 17th and 18th centuries, thanks to the Dutch East India Company, which explored and traded with Dutch colonies in Asia. Its many ships brought back a steady supply of exotic plants (some still living in the garden).

One of the most important plants brought back to Amsterdam by the Dutch East India Company was the Coffee Arabica plant, a plant that originated in Ethiopia. Because the Arab kings that dominated commerce in that area strictly controlled to whom coffee was sold, the company got hold of and smuggled coffee plants from an unknown location, eventually taking them back to the greenhouses at De Hortus, which were ideal to grow them. It is possible that a lot of the coffee in the world today had its origins in these plants!

Although quite small, De Hortus is home to over 6,000 plants from over 4,000 species. A different climate is represented in each of the seven greenhouses, so pretty much any plant from anywhere can grow there. Remember to close the sliding doors after you, as they're used to keep temperatures stable and to protect plants from diseases!

cool, yeah?

The oldest plant in De Hortus is the Eastern Cape giant cycad. It's over 300 years old, and counting!

Pharmacists, who conducted research in De Hortus alongside doctors, used to take their exams there.

In the 1930s, the Jewish Historical Museum was opened in Nieuwmarkt Square to teach people about Jewish and Dutch-Jewish life. The museum is spread out in four different former synagogues. The best way to learn about everyday Jewish life in Amsterdam is to visit the Children's Museum in the old Obbene Shul synagogue. The Children's Museum is built as the Hollander family home, so you get to navigate around and learn about the day-to-day of a Jewish family. You'll spend the day with Max, a tough-talking Matzo ball (a kind of Jewish bread) as he leads you through three floors of a Jewish family's home. It's a cool way to experience Jewish customs hands-on, like baking hallah (braided bread) and learning what kosher means in the kitchen, or playing an instrument in the music room.

This museum was closed during World War II when Germans occupied the city. Most of the collection was lost, but the items that were saved were used to slowly rebuild the museum, which eventually moved to the Ashkenazi complex. Part of the brick wall on the first floor landing was damaged during the war, and it's been left un-repaired on purpose. If it could talk, it would tell you so many stories about life through the centuries in the Jewish Quarter—some happy, some tragic. And this wall does talk!! It makes you stop and think...

cool, yeah?

JUNIOR
REALLY COOL!
JETSETTERS

Don't leave the building without trying all sorts of Jewish sweets in the colourful café downstairs!

The museum has more than 11,000 works of art, ceremonial items and historical objects. Only 5% of them are on permanent display.

cool, yEaH?

Robin Williams' wax figure is kissed by young girls so often that the paintwork needs to be retouched every now and again.

Some of the most popular figures are of Queen Beatrix of the Netherlands and her husband, but also Princess Maxima (who is more popular than the Queen!).

Where famous people stand oh-so-still for your photo...

A visit to Madame Tussauds wax museum is much more than just a chance to stand next to famous people (well, life-like recreations of famous people, anyway). It's also a great way to find out who these people really are (or were), what they did, and what they've contributed to the world.

You'll learn about some famous Dutch people, including Anne Frank—a Jewish girl who kept a diary about her experiences in hiding during World War II, and the artists Rembrandt and Vincent van Gogh. You'll also meet important figures who have truly changed the world, like the Dalai Lama (the highest spiritual leader of Tibetan Buddhism), Mikhail Gorbachev (the last president of the Soviet Union who ended the Cold War), Mahatma Gandhi (a leader who fought non-violently against injustice and oppression in India) and Nelson Mandela (the former president of South Africa known for his struggle against the segregation and discrimination of non-whites). But not everything is so serious. Many of the figures are of people you'll definitely recognize: Captain Jack Sparrow (Johnny Depp), Justin Timberlake, Robin Williams, Beyoncé Knowles, Brad Pitt, Oprah Winfrey and, of course, the person who started it all... Madame Tussaud herself!

visit over 700 animal species and make sure you bring home a super-star Artis de partis!

The Artis is the oldest zoo in the Netherlands and it's also the oldest park in Amsterdam. On the gigantic park grounds you'll find a tulip-packed botanical garden, a planetarium, a geological museum, an aquarium and a zoological museum, all in amazingly cute buildings dating back to the 19th century. There are vintage merry-go-rounds for those of you who are mild adventure seekers, and a reptile-and-butterfly house for those who're into a rush of adrenaline

The zoo is a mix of living animals and mounted exhibits about the animal kingdom. With over 700 species, you'll get a great overview of insects, amphibians, reptiles, fish, birds and mammals. For instance, check out the termite house. (The zoo had to build them a special safe house after they ate through the silicone on their old home and almost ran away!) Or, if you're wondering what might be lurking in the Amsterdam canals, check out the Aquarium for a replica of the muddy canal depths, including abandoned bikes that have been thrown in!

And don't forget to visit the Children's Farm to wander around with the domestic animals, many of which are traditional Dutch breeds, like Dutch land goats, belted calves, moorland sheep and tufted ducks. Artis has helped preserve some of them at a time when most have been replaced by higher-producing foreign breeds in modern farms.

cool, yEaH?

Before heading out, be sure to stop by the zoo's store and grab yourself a plush toy called Artis de Partis! He's the zoo's mascot and has some serious rock-star status in A'dam, although he's a bit like an old sock.

Natura Artist Magistra is Latin for 'nature is the teacher of art'. Artis is all Amsterdammers call it though!

a NEW CHURCH THAT ISN'T REALLY THAT NEW ANYMORE

The large church across the road from the Royal Palace is called De Nieuwe Kerk (The New Church)—but it isn't new at all! The areas that now make up the Netherlands converted to Christianity between the 6th and 9th centuries. Over the next few centuries, as the Catholic Church became more important, churches were built for the growing number of followers.

A large parish church was built in Amsterdam, but within a hundred years the population of the city had outgrown it. It was replaced by De Nieuwe Kerk (The New Church), while the original church became known as De Oude Kerk (The Old Church, SEE PAGE 56).

De Nieuwe Kerk is used for royal coronations and other royal events, but no longer for regular services. For such occasions the church is consecrated (declared sacred) before the ceremony and deconsecrated right after. The last time this happened was for the royal wedding of Prince Wilhelm and Princess Maxima.

cool, yEAH?

The church was almost completely destroyed in 1645 when plumbers accidentally started a fire.

Many of the Netherlands' naval heroes are buried inside this church. The most famous of all is Michiel de Ruyter, the country's most important Admiral. People like him were often called 'rich stinkers', because they could afford to be buried inside the church, but stank it up for all the other people!

a historic hangout place

In the late 15th century, a wall surrounded the city of Amsterdam. It had several gates for entering and leaving the city. One of these was St. Anthony's Gate (Sint Anthoniespoort). When the wall was taken down in the 17th century, the canals around it were land filled and a square was created to be used as a market place. This new market, *Nieuwmarkt* (or new market) would need a weighing house. Weighing scales were moved into the gate, at which point it became known as De Waag (which translates to 'the Weighing House'). That's the fortress-looking building you now see as the square's centrepiece. But De Waag didn't remain a weighing house for long. It became the guildhall

cool, yeah?

Jacob Hooy, which was a chemist shop when it opened in 1743, is still located in the exact same spot in the square. They now sell herbs and spices, teas, health food, homeopathic products, vitamins and health supplements.

for bricklayers, painters and surgeons (what a mix!). In the 18th century, a science theatre was built inside, where surgeons could perform public dissections of human corpses for the education of the crowds. It was also once home to the Amsterdam Historical Museum and the Jewish Historical Museum.

Today the Nieuwmarkt is a square near the edges of Amsterdam's Chinatown and Red Light districts, and the centre of the Nieuwmarktbuurt (Nieuwmarkt district). Cafés, terraces, coffee shops and canals surround it, and there's a weekly organic food market. These days in De Waag, you'll find a restaurant/café that's lit by 300 hundred candles!

an old church that really is old

De Oude Kerk, which was constructed over a 200 year period, was the first parish church in Amsterdam. During the Reformation, like many churches across the country, it became a Protestant church.

For a while the church also sheltered important documents, before they were moved to the city archive. The documents were kept in a chest covered in iron plates inside the Iron Chapel. To get in, you had to open three different locks, and three different people kept the keys! Mortar had to be removed from around the door by a mason and, once inside, one more locked door protected the chest. Talk about serious security!

Today, many events and concerts are held in the church. One of the favourite events is called 'Breakfast with Saskia'. Saskia van Uylenburgh and the painter Rembrandt registered their marriage here on 22 June 1634 (see page 62). The sacristy of the old church had a red door, which started the expression 'going through the red door'. It's what Amsterdammers sometimes say when they mean 'taking out a marriage license'. Saskia was buried here in 1642. Once a year the sun shines on her grave through a stained glass window and in between several of the church's columns. The management organizes a celebration at that exact time, with classical music at breakfast.

cool, yEaH?

Between the years 1300 (or so) and 1865, over 10,000 people were buried under the church. That's an average of 4 people stacked in each grave. If you look at the floor, you'll notice that it's made of about 2,500 gravestones! You can look them all up online! One of them was Dutch West India Company board member Kiliaen van Rensselaer, one of the founders of the New Amsterdam colony on Manhattan island – what we today call New York!

is it a museum? a house? a church? a chapel? a secret church hidden in an attic?

Even though it was originally a Catholic city, the Protestant religion flourished in Amsterdam during the 16th century. Before long, power shifted to the Protestants who passed a law that Catholic churches weren't allowed to face the street. But, this is where things get a little confusing. Even though it was technically forbidden to openly practise Catholicism, Amsterdam's policy was to tolerate different faiths. A wealthy Catholic merchant had an idea. He bought a canal house and two houses behind it and started renovating. The top three floors were converted into a Catholic church that was a 'secret' (although, really, people knew about it). At the time, it was actually one of the main Catholic churches in the city centre.

Years later the church was bought by a priest who made it more accessible by installing new stairs (and steep too!). After that, a large church (St. Nicolas) was built across the street and replaced Our Lord in the Attic as the local church. Since then it has become a museum. The church is over 350 years old, and visiting is like taking a trip back to the Golden Age of Amsterdam. Believe us, this is the coolest church you'll ever see. Be prepared to go up lots of stairs! And follow the lady bugs... they lead you to all the most interesting and interactive spots, just for kids!

cool, yeah?

The original name of the church was the Hart (Stag) because of a statue of a stag in front of the house.

a SERIOUSLY HUGE SYNAGOGUE

During the 16th and 17th centuries, some Sephardic Jews who were fleeing the Inquisition in Spain and Portugal came to Amsterdam and started a neighbourhood called the Jewish Quarter. Even though, at first, there were several different Sephardic Jewish communities, it wasn't long before they began co-operating and, by 1639, they formed the Talmud Torah: the Portuguese Jewish Community of Amsterdam.

Jews in the Dutch Republic had a lot of freedom of religion—something that was pretty unique at the time. And, in 1670, the wealthy Portuguese Jewish community decided to buy a site to build a huge synagogue. It was completed within five years. Smaller buildings surrounded the synagogue and were used for social and charity purposes.

The beautiful Esnoga (an old Portuguese word for synagogue) has been the inspiration for many synagogues since it was built. They include some in London, England; Naarden, the Netherlands; Newport, Rhode Island; and New York, USA. Attention: this is still a synagogue where people come to worship. When you visit, wear appropriate clothes (nothing too flashy or skimpy). Boys will be asked to wear a *yamukah* on their heads out of respect.

cool, yEaH?

The floor is covered with fine sand that absorbs dust, moisture and dirt. It also reduces noise.

The building stands on wooden poles that can still be seen by boat from the canals which used to border the Jewish Quarter.

To learn some more: Sephardic Jews are those that originated from the Iberian Peninsula (Spain, Portugal, Morocco, Andorra and also Gibraltar). Ashkenazi Jews originated in the west of Germany, many of whom migrated to Russia or Eastern Europe. Mazrahi Jews descend from those in the Middle East, North Africa, Central Asia and the Caucasus.

Get your artistic inspiration from the great master himself

Rembrandt Harmenszoon van Rijn was a Dutch painter and etcher who lived and worked in Amsterdam. In 1639, he bought his first house with his dear wife, Saskia van Uylenburg. It was so expensive that he was only able to pay for it in instalments—even though he was making a lot of money (something that was rare for an artist)! That was mostly because he was also a successful art dealer. Rembrandt's studio was on the second floor, where he liked to work undisturbed. In the attic he kept a small but expensive collection of exotic relics from all over the world. Despite his fame and wealth, Rembrandt was eventually unable to pay what he still owed on the house. He declared bankruptcy and his house and every single one of his possessions were auctioned off. Can you imagine how horrible it must have been to lose his house and his beloved collection? This, as well as the death of his wife Saskia, caused him great pain, and that feeling comes across in that period's paintings. Rembrandt is most famous for his paintings, such as *The Night Watch*, *The Jewish Bride*, and many portraits and self-portraits. But he was also an expert in etching and printmaking. When you visit the museum, you'll learn how etchings were printed in the 17th century. Or, if painting is more your thing, the staff will show you how paint was made in Rembrandt's time.

REMBRANDT HOUSE MUSEUM
Museum het Rembrandthuis

cool, yeah?

Rembrandt was a collector of exotic art and curiosities from all over the world, including rare shells, corals, feathers, stones and exotic arms.

Like many master painters of his time, Rembrandt had a lot of pupils (at least 40!), who often earned by copying the master's works!

MUSEUM HET REMBRANDTHUIS

The Golden Age Captured in Brush Strokes

The Night Watch is the most famous work you'll see at the Rijksmuseum. Painted by Rembrandt in 1642, it shows Captain Frans Banning Cocq with his lieutenant, Willem van Ruytenburch and their company. What really makes the painting interesting though are the stories that surround it. For example, it's called *The Night Watch* because of a layer of varnish that made it look like a night scene, until it was removed in the 1940s. Also, what you'll see isn't exactly what Rembrandt painted. The canvas was once larger, but was probably trimmed by a former owner so it would fit into a smaller frame. In 1975, a disturbed man attacked the painting with a knife. In 1990, another man threw acid at it. Both times, the painting was almost fully restored, but it's now kept under close watch. There are often lineups for this one, so if you want to see the painting, try to get there early! You can learn more about it on page 16.

The museum also has a large collection of works from the Dutch Golden Age—a time when the Netherlands was the most wealthy and powerful country on earth. To make your visit to the museum into a game, buy Gordon the Warden materials at the information desk and search for five of the museum's masterpieces!

Cool, yeah?

The Rijksmuseum's permanent collection has over 1 million pieces, one of the largest in the world!

There's a copy of 'The Night Watch' in the National Gallery in London, which shows the way the painting looked originally.

a REally Edgy museum... inside a flying bath tub!

The Stedelijk Museum is Amsterdam's contemporary art museum. Like with many modern art museums, people often disagree about the artistic choices the museum makes. The original building was built to house a collection of art and antiques that one person donated to the city. Her name was Sophia Augusta Lopez Suasso de Bruyn and she was considered to be quite eccentric. In 1938 the Stedelijk became the state museum of modern art. The building is unique, with a neo-renaissance look—a real contrast to the modern art inside. It has been undergoing big renovations for several years and is set to reopen in late 2009. When the renovations are done, the new addition will double the size of the museum, and will double its reputation for controversy and eccentricity! The addition pops out of one of the wings of the old building and looks like a gigantic flying white bath tub! It's also going to be full of cool stuff for kids to explore.

Inside the bath tub you'll be able to see many types of art (from Impressionism to Fauvism, from Cubism to Espressionism), by artists like Henri Matisse, Pablo Picasso and Andy Warhol. In addition to paintings, the collection includes sculptures, photos, films and videos, installation art (art that aims to change the way you experience a particular space), books and furniture. Many of the works are being displayed in various places across Amsterdam until the new building opens.

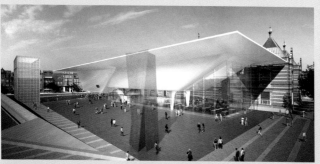

cool, yeah?

In 1973, a significant part of the Stedelijk Museum's collection left to create the Van Gogh Museum!

Pack yourself a picnic and get ready for the Vondel!

In 1864, a group of Amsterdam citizens got together to raise money for a park on the edge of the city. Nieuwe Park opened with grassy areas, ponds and paths for strolling or riding horses. Before long, a new feature was added: a statue of Joost van den Vondel, a famous Dutch writer and playwright, and the whole place was eventually named Vondelpark in his honour. As the city grew, Vondelpark grew, too, and became the city's most popular green space. There's always something up, so check out its website!

Every day, the park is packed with people walking, jogging, rollerblading, walking their dogs, listening to music or just relaxing. They go to the restaurants, the open-air theatre, and the National Film Museum, screening old and new flicks. And every year Queen's Day is celebrated in Vondelpark big time! On this holiday, people Dutch-up by putting up flags to show their support for Queen Beatrix, and orange is seen all over the country. (Orange is the national colour, and also the colour of the Queen's family, the House of Orange-Nassau.) It's a day of national unity... and, of course, there's plenty of yummy food and lots of music.

cool, yEaH?

One of the sculptures in the park, called 'The Fish', was made by Pablo Picasso in 1965.

Vondelpark has six play areas and one large playground near Groot Melkhuis. You can stop by seven days of the week and not be bored!

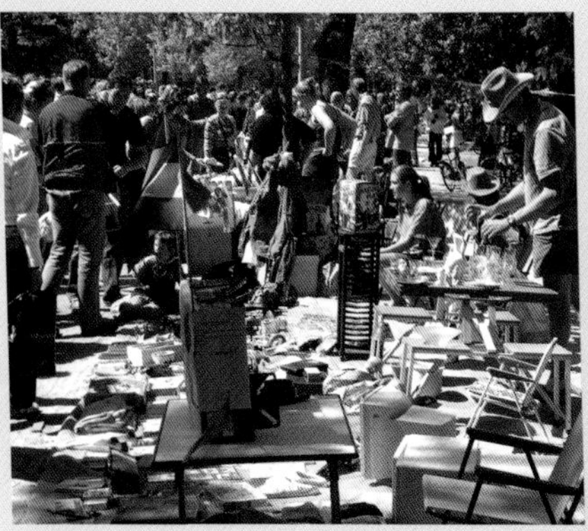

ONCE OLD FACTORIES, NOW A CREATIVE, CULTURAL COMMUNITY

In the late 19th century, a factory was built in Westerpark to provide gas for lighting the streets and buildings of Amsterdam. It was the largest coal plant in the country and was made up of gas refineries, a water tower and offices. But when natural gas was discovered in the north, the factory closed down. Part of it was demolished and what remained was used mainly for storage. The area had been badly polluted but was eventually cleaned up, and the remaining buildings were recognized as industrial monuments—which saved them from being torn

down and turned them into really interesting places! The property and many buildings were used for cultural activities like festivals, shows, operas and even circus acts. Then, in 2003, the area was revamped and finally became a large park. The buildings are being updated for future use, and some are already home to a few really neat things! There's space for so many activities. People come to have picnics, to go skateboarding, to play ball or just to hang out and relax. In some of the old factory buildings there are also restaurants, cafés, shops, galleries and even a cinema that shows the latest movies—mostly Dutch and European.

cool, yEaH?

If you come by early in the morning, you'll notice the scent of freshly-baked bread from a bakery on site. Yummy! (Make sure you get to try some of it!)

THE TALLEST TOWER IN TOWN

The Protestant religion has been practised in the Netherlands and in Europe since the Renaissance. At that time, Protestants mostly lived in the north of the country, and Catholics mostly lived in the south, and the two groups didn't always get along too well.

As the Protestant religion grew more and more popular, many churches were built. One of them was the Westerkerk. This Gothic-style church has the tallest tower in all of Amsterdam. It stands 85 metres (279 feet) high. On top of the tower is the coat of arms of the Imperial Crown of Austria donated by Emperor Maximilian, who was from the powerful Habsburg royal line. At the time, this family ruled Austria, Spain, and parts of the Lower Countries, including the Netherlands.

When the independence of the Netherlands was recognized in 1648, seven Protestant provinces and one Roman Catholic came together: this was finally the Netherlands.

The country became known for its religious tolerance, allowing people to worship whoever or however they wished as long as their practice didn't disturb other people's right to do the same. As a result, the country became a refuge for Jews, Puritans and Huguenots fleeing less friendly parts of Europe. After World War II, major religions began to decline, and in today's society religion plays only a lesser role.

cool, yeah?

Westerkerk is the resting place of the painter Rembrandt.

The hour bell in the tower is the heaviest in Amsterdam, weighing over 7,500 kg.

HITCH A RIDE ON A WINDMILL

What's big, goes round and round, and is as Dutch as it gets? Nope… it's not an elephant wearing clogs on a carousel. It's a windmill, of course. Windmills are machines that harness the energy of the wind, and the Netherlands is famous for them. They even celebrate National Windmill Day! Because Amsterdam is below sea level, it has always been important that the city had a way to remove water in case of floods—and windmills are perfect for this. There are eight windmills left in Amsterdam, but only one of them is open to the public and still works. They all had different purposes, like moving water, sawing wood, milling grain into flour or extracting oil from seeds. The Molen van Sloten

(Sloten Windmill) is a windmill that pumps water out of the area. The city continues to pay the miller (the person who works the windmill) for the amount of water pumped! During your visit, you'll climb up to the top of the windmill and see how it all works. The Coopery Museum is attached to the windmill—you can see traditional Dutch crafts and clothing. And if you're in Amsterdam on the 2nd Sunday of August, you're in for a real treat. 'Sloten on its Head' is your sole chance to take a ride on the sails of a real windmill (the miller will tie you on, and off you go). Dutch people often call millers 'land sailors' since they are in charge of operating the windmills' sails and worry about the weather all the time. And even though the other seven are closed, you can still stop by to have a look!

cool, yeah?

At one time, there were over 10,000 windmills in the Netherlands. Today there are only about 1,000—of those only 500 are still working. Pig fat and beeswax are still used to lubricate the equipment. These old types of grease are more effective than any modern lubricants!

MUSIC HITS AND YUMMINNESS FROM ALL OVER THE WORLD

The music most North Americans and Western Europeans are familiar with can be considered western. But western music makes up only a small portion of all the music made across the world. The Amsterdam Roots Festival is a week-long celebration of global music and culture that happens in mid-June.

Roots Open Air normally kicks off the event. Five stages present music from different ethnic backgrounds, influences and styles from all over the world: Zap City (music from big cities around the world), Couleur Locale (music by Dutch newcomers), Urban Groove (music by young Dutch artists), Samba Stage (Brazilian and samba music) and Kids@Roots (music by young artists).

The music you can hear is as diverse as the people that now live in and visit Amsterdam. It includes traditional (folk) music, art music, popular (pop) music, regional music and fusion music. So turn off your iPod and spend a few hours mingling with the international crowd at Oosterpark. You might discover a sound you've never heard before, and for sure some yummy food you don't often get a chance to taste! And there are also hundreds of kids to play with in the fun areas and kids' shows!

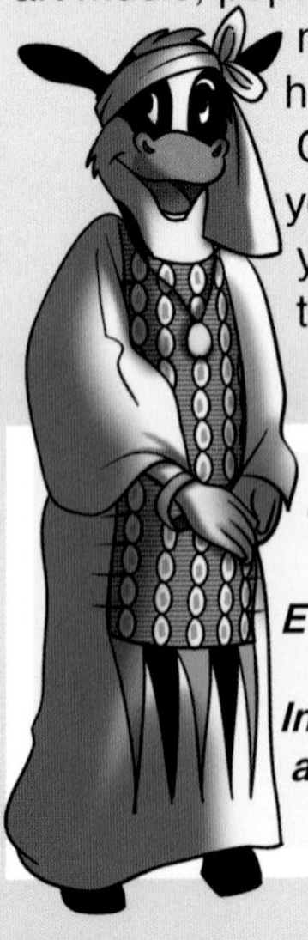

COOL, YEAH?

Every year the festival has a different theme.

In 2007 the Amsterdam Roots Festival attracted 65,000 visitors. Stop by next time!

BLOEDWORST
BERE
VLEESWORST
FLADDER
MAIS
TELLO
BLOEDWORST

HOP ON YOUR BIKE AND DON'T FORGET YOUR HELMET!

Amsterdam is often called the bike capital of the world, and there's a good reason! Almost half of the traffic in the city is bike traffic. In fact, the city is so bicycle-friendly that Amsterdammers can be seen riding rain or shine. There is a huge network of safe and quick bicycle routes with their own lanes, traffic signs and signals. The city continues to improve and extend its network of routes and bike parking garages, like the huge multi-storey one you'll see just outside Central Station (SEE PAGE 78). Most of the bikes in the city look old, scratched and dented. This is partly because they're used so much. But it's also because everyone assumes that their bike will be stolen at some point (thousands of bikes are stolen every month) and they figure that, if they have an old one, it won't draw as much attention.

If you want to see the city like the Amsterdammers do, going by bike is definitely one of the best ways! Renting a bike is easy, and you'll probably get a choice: a shiny new bike, a typical Amsterdam bike, or even a decorated one. Why not choose one that's all beat up, for a true Amsterdam experience?

cycliNG RulEs + safEty tips

1. The Dutch rarely wear helmets (because they mess up their nice hair-dos), but you should!!
2. Get familiar with the bike lanes and use a map.
3. Pay attention to the signs and follow the rules.
4. Give trams the right of way.
5. Signal using your hands.
6. Pay attention to what's around you.
7. Always lock your bike when you park.
8. Keep moving with other bicyclists and walk your bike on crowded streets or in pedestrian zones.
9. Avoid tram tracks.
10. If it rains, be extra careful on Amsterdam's old and slippery streets.

go by 'boot'! ahoy, canal sailor!

Because of its cool canal system, Amsterdam is often called 'The Venice of the North'. The city has over 100 kilometres of canals with about 90 islands and 1,500 bridges. And what better way to see them all than by boat? (Or by *boot*, if you feel like speaking Dutch.) There are lots of options: breakfast, lunch or dinner cruises; music cruises; theatre cruises and theme cruises. There are also hop-on and hop-off cruises that let you discover all the sights the city has to offer.

How did all those canals come to be? During the Golden Age (17th century), tons of people were immigrating to Amsterdam. All these new people needed new homes. And they needed to eat, so new shops had to be opened to sell them food and other items. City officials decided to build the canals so that all of these new buildings could be made accessible for people by boat, the main means of transporting cargo back then. One canal already existed in the city—the Singel. It started out as a moat to help defend the city against intruders. The other three canals—Herengracht (Gentleman's Canal), Keizersgracht (Emperor's Canal) and Prinsengracht (Prince's Canal)—were built especially to accommodate all the new residents of the city. Another canal (Nassau/Stadhouderskade), which is farther out, was made for defense and water management. Smaller canals connect these main canals throughout the city, totalling a whopping 100 km of waterways and forming 90 islands connected by 1,500 bridges!!

canal boats
Grachtenboten rondvaarten

cool, yeah?

Looking at the map you would think that the canals were built from the centre, out, but they weren't! They were built from the west to the east.

Amsterdam's first pleasure cruise happened in 1621 when Queen Elisabeth Stuart of Bohemia visited.

follow a canal through a'dam

Canals make up about 25 percent of the city! They were first built for both water management and defense. But, as the city grew, newer defensive canals were built, and older ones gradually became important transportation routes. A large number of canals were built during the Golden Age, fanning out from the city centre. Their construction created many islands and countless bridges (see pages 38, 80 and 130). Many of the original canals were filled in over time to create new land. But the ones that remain are used for travel around the city, mostly by a canal-bus system. Festivals and parades are often held on the waters, too. And in the winter, when the canals freeze, people skate on them! There are old paintings in Amsterdam's museums showing that people have been skating-crazy since the Golden Age!

Walking alongside the canals is a great way to see the city. As you walk past neighbourhoods, you'll get a feel for life in different areas, and as many Dutch people dislike curtains, you'll also get a sneak-peak into dozens of living rooms! On hot summer days Amsterdammers put out their lounge chairs on the entrance landings of their building, or even in a parking spot by the canal side, and chill-out in the sun. On these days Amsterdam feels like a village, as everyone is extra-friendly. Boaters wave at the people, who wave back at them, or raise one finger only (which in Holland means 'hi'). You can pick a spot around the Amstel to watch boats be lifted up and down in the locks, or bridges be raised for taller yachts. And watch for houseboats. (You can spot them by looking for bikes, vases or clothes lines on the deck.) The canals are lined with cafés, restaurants, and even markets, such as the Bloemenmarkt (see page 86).

cool, yEaH?

The canals are flushed 3 times a week to help keep them clean. A network of locks allows water to flow in from the IJmeer.

There are about 20 different species of fish and crabs living in the canals. You can see how that looks at the Artis Zoo** (SEE PaGE 50)**.

YOUR ONE AND ONLY CHANCE TO EAT PANCAKES FOR DINNER!

Pannekoeken are the Dutch version of pancakes. The batter used to make them is a lot like pancake batter, but that's where the similarities end! Pannekoeken are egg-rich, puffy, thinner and larger than the typical American pancake. But don't confuse them with French crêpes! Pannekoeken are thicker and larger. And, most Dutch would swear to you that they're also much, much yummier. Pannekoeken aren't a breakfast food in Amsterdam, either! They're usually eaten for lunch or dinner. Servings are generous, so unless you're starving, you might want to share an order. *Poffertjes* are another traditional Dutch treat—a bit like mini-pancakes served with powdered sugar or butter, but way sweeter. Inside, they're also softer. They're prepared in special cast-

COOL, YEAH?

You can have your dinner time pancake sweet, savoury or stuffed—the choice is yours. You can pick fillings like sliced apples, cheese, ham, bacon or candied ginger... or go with a Dutch classic filling: bacon and 'stroop' (a thick syrup).

iron trays where many can be cooked at the same time. Many restaurants in Amsterdam have pannekoeken and poffertjes on their menus, so you could fork a couple after lunch, anytime. But the best place, by far, to enjoy a real, genuine one is at a *pannekoekenhuis* (pancake house). The selection can't be beat. Keep in mind that pannekoeken can be either sweet or savoury (salty). Traditional sweet pannekoeken include apple-sugar-cinnamon, raisin and sugar, powder sugar, sugar syrup and plain sugar. Traditional savoury pannekoeken are made with ham, cheese, or whatever the chef decides to put on the menu to surprise you. If you're visiting in the summer, Junior Jetsetters also suggests checking out De Vier Pilaren, a small canal-side wooden restaurant just outside Leidseplein (look for the Night Watch-inspired restaurant sign—SEE PAGE 16).

would you trade your house for a tulip? it's a no-brainer...

Amsterdam and the Netherlands are known for many things, including canals and flowers (particularly tulips). The Bloemenmarkt combines both these things into one experience, and has been doing so for over a hundred years! The flower stalls stand on houseboats here, in the Singel canal. This floating flower market is the only one in the world. There are thousands of seeds, bulbs, flowers, bouquets and pot plants to choose from, as well as souvenirs. If you have a green thumb, stop by and pick up your supply of seeds and bulbs for the season—if you're allowed to bring them home—and pick up a pair of clogs while you're at it! Tulips originated in Central Asia and were first cultivated by the Turks, perhaps as far back as the

11th century. They didn't reach the Netherlands until the 17th century, when a biologist who was the director of De Hortus (SEE PAGE 44) received some flower bulbs from the Dutch Ambassador to Constantinople (now called Istanbul, the capital of Turkey). It didn't take long for a craze called 'Tulipmania' to start. Traders made huge amounts of money and people began selling their businesses, homes, farm animals and whatever else they could to be involved in this new industry. Eventually, a 'Tulip Crash' occurred when an over-supply led to many people going bankrupt and losing everything they had! This didn't deter the Dutch, though! People still love fresh flowers, and that's really the only thing you will see in Amsterdam more often than bicycles. Sometimes you'll see people riding their bikes with a bunch of flowers under their arm!

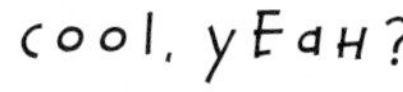

The Netherlands exports two-thirds of all fresh-cut plants, flowers and bulbs you see in every flower shop in the world. Now that's a lot of flowers!

At the height of Tulipmania, some varieties of tulips could cost more than an entire house in Amsterdam—and Amsterdam houses were never cheap!

a floating music festival

The Grachtenfestival is a classical music lover's dream. This annual festival takes place all over the centre of the city in different important places that have architectural, cultural or historical value. The concerts are also often performed on boats in the canals or in private homes. The music, and there's a lot of it—about 90 concerts in all!—isn't the only feature of the festival, though. Canal tours and architecture and monument walks/tours are also part of it. It combines two important parts of Amsterdam life: high culture and water. The Grachtenfestival was inspired by the Prinsengracht

Concert, which is held outside the Hotel Pulitzer. This is one cool concert venue on a pontoon boat in the canal! It's still the main event of the festival. Come early because you'll want a good view of the canal! But be prepared to stand, since there are no seats... Other concerts and events in the festival are smaller. Whatever event you go to, though, it's sure to be an unforgettable experience. Even if you think classical music is only for grannies (and there are a lot of grannies there), give it a go. How often do you get to see a whole orchestra performing Mozart on a floating platform in a canal? Seriously, don't miss out on it!

cool, yeah?

The Kindergrachtenfestival has a stage specifically for kids, with music for all ages—from babies to teenagers. Even if the main concerts aren't your thing, you'll like some of these!

take the tram through a'dam!

There are tons of ways to get around Amsterdam: by bus, metro, train, ferry, taxi or rickshaw. But the best way—the Amsterdammer way—is to take the trams. They make their way through the winding streets and over the countless canals. As they pass, you'll hear their unique and familiar sounds: the heavy metallic rolling of the wheels on the tracks, and those screeching bells warning people to get out of the way. All of Amsterdam's trams depart from Centraal Station (or CS—see page 34) and go southward, half of them on an eastern route, and half on a western route.

But before you hop on, there are a few things to know. Even though all trams have a driver, only some have a conductor (wearing burgundy uniforms). If there's a conductor, board at the door where he or she sits. This will either be the second door from the back if the tram is a shiny new one, or at the far back if it's an older one. Once on board, you can either buy a single fare ticket or be smart like the locals and buy a strippenkaart (or strip card) in advance. A strippenkaart is a ticket with 15 strips that you stamp as you go. You'll have to show it to the conductor and say 'naar Centraal Station', for instance. The conductor will then stamp the right number of strips. If there's no conductor, you can use any door. Press the button to open the door and then stamp your ticket right away (in the city centre 2 strips are usually enough, or 3 if you're going a bit further). Just check your last stamp, fold the strippenkaart right after the last strip you need for your ride, and stamp it. Sounds complicated, but it's really very easy!

And if you're really into trams, there's even a museum dedicated to them. The Electrische Museumtramlijn Amsterdam has trams from all over Europe, between the years 1910–1960. But the point is to experience tram travel, not just to look at old trams! Many still work and travel along a 7 km line with 14 stops, just for your enjoyment!

14

10
Van Hallstraat
7

cool, yeah?

JUNIOR
REALLY COOL!
JETSETTERS

There are 80.5 km of tram tracks and 81.2 km of metro tracks.

Amsterdam has 236 blue-and-white GVB trams, which can go as fast as 70 km/h.

NATIONALE STRIPPEN KAART
EUR 6,90
1
2
3
4
5
6
7
8
9
10
11
12
13
14
15
STRIPPENKAART ONGEVOUWEN TONEN
• Alleen een strippenkaart met een leesbare, te controleren stempelafdruk is geldig.
• Na een tariefwijziging is deze strippenkaart nog twaalf maanden geldig.
• Meer informatie vindt u op de achterzijde van deze kaart of surf naar: www.ov-info.nl

Ride a ferry or stuff your face with pancakes and stroop

Behind Centraal Station, there are three ferries that head to Amsterdam Noord (North Amsterdam). On the left, the ferry to NDSM Werf is the longest crossing, giving you the chance to enjoy a great view of Amsterdam from the water. The ferry to Buiksloterweg in the middle is the shortest and goes directly across the river. The ferry to IJplein on the right goes to a residential area in the north. Even though there isn't a lot to do on the other side, the free ferry rides there and back are enough reason to go! Just be sure to bring your camera! There are also cruises on the IJ and in the harbour

that will give you a glimpse of the more industrial side of Amsterdam. See, up close, how the big ships move and manoeuvre; how they're pushed around narrow areas by tiny (and powerful) tugboats, and guided by pilot boats. Find out how they dock, how they're loaded and unloaded, and prepared for departure. You could easily watch this fascinating stuff for hours in this busy port. You can also see some of this happening on the NDSM Werf. For a uniquely Dutch experience, hop on the Pannenkoekenboot. These boat rides combine two very Dutch things: pancakes and cruises. What better way could there be to enjoy the IJ than while eating delicious pannekoeken (SEE PaGE 84)?!

cool, yEaH?

The cruises on the Pannenkoekenboot offer all-you-can-eat pancakes. So make sure you're hungry! And you think maple syrup is good? On this boat that's just the beginning. You can also choose toppings like cheese, ham, fruit, jam and chocolate sprinkles, and the stroop syrup is yummy!

Head out the back doors for a whole new Amsterdam look

Most people who visit Amsterdam arrive at Centraal Station, go out the front doors that open onto the Damrak, and stay around the historic canals. But for something different, head out the back of the station. You'll be greeted by Het IJ (the river) and Amsterdam Noord (North Amsterdam) on the opposite bank. You can go east toward the Eastern Docklands from here (or take a ferry across—SEE PAGE 92). Walking along the water of the Eastern Docklands is an alternative to the canals, and gives you a completely different experience. The area is much more open. Gigantic freight and cruise ships move slowly in every direction. When you leave the station, you'll pass a large floating Chinese restaurant, and a magic theatre boat. Crossing the footbridge

will take you to NEMO and the Eastindiaman Amsterdam… But because you are in Amsterdam, instead of stopping at a red light, you might have to stop while the bridge opens to let a tall boat pass. Behind NEMO, lots of inhabited antique house-boats are docked, some of which are part of the Maritime Museum's collection. Continuing along the Eastern Docklands will take you to the Oostenburgervaart and Wittenburgervaart neighourhoods, both developed over the past few years. Here, you'll find small shops, artist studios and small communities all over. The area is actually made up of several islands and peninsulas in the IJmeer, with bridges connecting them to both the mainland and to one another. The best part is that the entire area is made for walking and biking, with kilometres of quiet roads and paths.

COOL, YEAH?

During the Middle Ages, this area didn't exist at all, except for a few small islands. All the land you see was created by the city.

FROM RAGS TO RICHES AND STYLE

During the Golden Age, Amsterdam was expanding, and an area called the Jordaan was added. It was mostly made up of poor immigrants—Flemish, newly-arrived Spanish and Portuguese Jews and French Huguenots (members of the Protestant Reformed Church). It was extremely overcrowded with tiny houses packed with lots of families. Back then, the Jordaan wasn't a nice place to live at all. The canals were used for transportation and sewage and there was no running water for daily use. Today, the area has changed dramatically. The slums have turned into a hip area popular with artists,

students and young professionals. The narrow streets and canals are filled with galleries, courtyards, unique boutiques, small museums and historic homes. Noorderkerk (North Church), in the Noordermarkt (North Market), is the main church in the area, although the Westerkerk (SEE PAGE 72) is also here. Over the years the area has been home to some notable people, including Rembrandt and Anne Frank and her family, who hid for over two years during World War II in one of Jordaan's houses. It's one of the best places in the city to feel the pulse of normal day-to-day life in Amsterdam, shop for unique clothes and souvenirs, or just walk in the sun!

cool, yEaH?

In 1900, when it was an overcrowded neighbourhood, about 80,000 people lived in the Jordaan. Today there are only 20,000 inhabitants.

Look for the stone tablets above the doors to many local buildings. They'll tell you the profession of the person who first lived there (e.g. a pair of scissors means a tailor).

catch an EERiE choral concert

Like most churches, the Church of St. Nicholas has an organ often used during mass. Every Saturday, a choral evensong is sung. This is a religious (Anglican) gathering where a choir sings most of the service. The church has three full choirs, so there's never a shortage of singers.

As well as being used for church services, St. Nicolaaskerk also hosts concerts. But not just any concerts. They specialize in choral and instrumental music. And it's a great place for this kind of music. The inside of the church is nicely decorated, and the acoustics and pipe organ are amazing. Besides, because concerts are usually held after dusk, there's an eerie, mysterious coolness about it!

The church's Sauer organ is one of the finest in the Netherlands. Every summer, during the International Organ Concert Series, well-known organists from all over the world (including the Netherlands, of course) come to Amsterdam to play it. It's quite impressive to see them up there!

cool, yeah?

The church is not typical for a Roman Catholic church. Most of those, at that time, were built in the neo-Gothic style, while the Church of St. Nicholas is neo-Baroque. It's really huge inside!

youR blockbustERs iN stylE!!

The Pathé Tuschinski Cinema was the fifth cinema built by Abraham Icek Tuschinski—a Dutch businessman. Tuschinski came to the city from Poland at a time when movies were becoming a new craze, and he saw a great opportunity. The theatre is built in the Art Nouveau and Art Deco styles and is nothing like the ones you're probably used to. Tuschinski spared no expense and made it really fancy. He was trying to attract customers who were used to the luxury of royal theatres and grand opera houses, and had rarely been to the movies. It's also big! This is because he needed space for musicians. Silent cinema was still all the rage at the time, and musicians were needed to accompany the on-screen action. (Can you imagine how boring it would have been without any sound?) The cinema has a magnificent entrance and two tall towers that rise above any of the other buildings in the

cool, yEaH?

The maze of corridors was meant to provide privacy to the early patrons.

The main theatre is smaller than the original, but private boxes are still available, so why not splurge a bit and watch your flick in big style...?

neighbourhood. Inside, the main theatre used to have a stage, an organ and even a resident orchestra with 16 members. There were two balconies, and private suites for the wealthiest—something not often seen in a cinema. During World War II, Tuschinski and his family (who were Jewish), were killed in a concentration camp. The cinema was seized and its name was changed to Tivoli. After the war, the original name returned. The cinema underwent some changes, and a new wing was added. It's now part of the Pathé cinema network and shows all kinds of movies—from American blockbusters to Dutch cinema, in both languages. Be sure to catch a film there, and go in early to walk around the building. Who knows, maybe you'll even bump into a celebrity or two since most of the movie premieres in the Netherlands are held at the Pathé Tuschinski. It's by far the most beautiful cinema you'll ever munch popcorn in!

an artistic extravaganza

The Uitmarkt ('out market')—the three-day opening of the new Dutch cultural season—is an artistic extravaganza. Every year in late August, events go on all over the city centre. You'll find art everywhere, from museum walls to street corners. It's one big party with exhibitions, shows, art studio previews and workshops. Over 2,000 artists perform in open concerts, and there's something for everyone of every age with previews of theatre, cabaret, dance, opera, mime, children's theatre, street theatre, literary readings and film. All kinds of music can be heard, such as pop, classical,

cool, yeah?

Maybe you've heard the saying 'getting on your soap box.' Well, at the Uitmarkt they take it seriously. Street artists advertise themselves on real soapboxes!

hip-hop, jazz, gospel, world, funk, DJ, rock… the list just goes on and on. The best places to be at are Amsterdam's main squares, like Rembrandtplein (SEE PAGE 16), Waterlooplein (SEE PAGE 104), Leidseplein or Nieuwmarkt (SEE PAGE 54) where people tend to gather. And, of course, like any street party, there are lots of food vendors everywhere. Yummy! One of the other highlights is the book market. Hundreds of publishers present their new books, while booksellers show off their collections of used, antique and hard-to-find books. You'll even find some English books! (Or you could just brush up on your Dutch skills!)

Shop around for old bicycle wheels, orange T-shirts and a pair of yellow clogs

Markets have been part of Amsterdam since the 18th century when the first stall was set up in the Jewish Quarter. Today, there are many different markets. Some are open daily, some one or two days a week and some only on certain days of the season or year.

The Bloemenmarkt, or Flower Market (see page 86) is one of the most unique. For anyone interested in antiques, there's the Antiekmarkt De Looier, which also has curious objects. It's one of the few markets that is covered. The Art Plein Spui is great if you want to pick up some original artwork, including prints and small oil paintings. For book lovers, there's the amazing Boekenmarkt, featuring books, cards and maps. (You might even feel like you're back in the Middle Ages in those dark alleys.) Collectors of stamps, coins, old postcards and medals will have a blast at the Postzegelmarkt.

The Waterlooplein Flea Market is by far the largest, and has a huge assortment of items among its 300 stands. It's also the most popular with younger people, with T-shirts, posters, spray paint for graffiti and a lot of Dutch things that you can't even. And if you're looking for yummy Dutch food, try the Farmer's Market on the Noordermarkt and a weekly market in the Nieuwmarkt (see page 54), both specializing in organic foods, fresh fruits, cheese, cakes and snacks.

Some tips before you head out: most of the items have been individually priced and this price is usually fixed. If you want to try haggling, then the Waterlooplein is your best bet. Elsewhere, people might sometimes take offense. And beware of pickpockets by keeping one eye on your belongings (just in case)!

cool, yeah?

It's all about haggling, so drive your hardest bargain. You're sure to get a great discount, but you might have to call the seller's bluff! If you're looking to buy, arrive early to get first pick.

the dam that stopped the sea

The Zuiderzee was once a salt water inlet of the North Sea with rough and dangerous waters. That's why, in 1918, the Zuiderzee Act was passed in Parliament, with three goals: to protect the area from the North Sea; to increase food supply by creating new farmlands; and to create a lake to improve water management. The plan also called for several smaller projects, with Afsluitdijk (the Closure Dike) being the most important. The dike is a dam that completely separates the Zuiderzee from the North Sea. Once the Closure Dike was finished, new land was created by pumping water out of the newly-created lake (called the IJsselmeer).

The resulting new lands (or polders) are called Wieringermeer, Noordoostpolder and Flevoland. You can learn more about the Zuiderzee at the Zuiderzeemuseum (SEE PAGE 130). In addition to creating a lake, the Closure Dike also connects North Holland to the northern province of Friesland. It runs 32 km (20 miles) through the water, a lake on one side, the sea on the other. There is lots of landscape to see along the way. Stop at the car parks to get a great view, or bike across! About half way in there's even a small village called Breezanddijk—first created for the construction workers who built the dike. Today, only a handful of people live there and the only store is a gas station!

cool, yeah?

The polders that were created added about 165,000 hectares (or 2,323 km^2) and are home to about 430,000 people.

During World War II, the German Army tried to seize the Afsluitdijk, but they failed.

cool, yEaH?

The Alkmaar cheese carrier's guild has been bringing cheese buyers and sellers together since 1593!

Mild cheeses are aged for 4 to 6 weeks, medium cheeses are aged 8 to 12 weeks, matured cheeses are aged 12 to 18 weeks, aged cheeses are aged 6 to 12 months, and extra-aged cheese are aged for more than one year!

Say Cheeeeeese!!!

The Dutch are famous for their cheese. In fact, the Netherlands is often thought of as ***the*** cheese country. It's not all that surprising when you start to notice how many dairy cows they have there (more than people, it seems). If you drive through the Dutch countryside in the summertime you should be able to smell them!

Milk, in its untreated form, doesn't last long. This was especially true centuries ago when people didn't know about pasteurization. So what were they supposed to do with all that milk? And how could they transport it great distances without it spoiling on the way? The answer, of course, was… cheese! And with all that cheese hanging around, it wasn't long before markets were created to sell it.

Today there are five such markets in the Netherlands. Of these, four are reproductions of the traditional markets from the Middle Ages. (Yes, cheese has been around for a very long time!) One of them is Alkmaar, where you can see demonstrations of how these markets were once operated. In Alkmaar, teams of cheese porters (called *kaasdragers*) bring large wheels of cheese (*kaasrij*) on wooden barrows to and from a traditional weighing house. There are normally about 160 kg (350 pounds) of cheese on each barrow. The merchants will show you how they sampled the cheeses back then, and decided on a price. You'll learn about the barter system they used, which was called *handjeklap* ('clapping hands'). Don't forget to bring your camera (then get ready to say 'cheese!'). This is one of the most photo-friendly events you'll see, and everyone is kitted in full traditional gear! When you're done, don't forget to check out the rest of Alkmaar. You'll love its cute historic centre... Start with the Cheese Museum!

take a wild Ride inside yourself

The human body is like a sophisticated machine. From the control room, it monitors the temperature, water level, food digestion and heartbeat. All of this is done by trillions of cells instructed by the brain—the body's most impressive organ. Even the most powerful of computers couldn't handle that much information at that speed!

But how does your body actually work? And what does it look like from the inside? The Corpus Experience will give you the details. Corpus isn't a museum—it's a 'journey through the human body'. The building is even shaped like a sitting human body! Experience the life of a red blood cell, or discover how the food you ate at lunch gets digested by your stomach and intestines before, you know, coming out the other side.

At Corpus, you'll learn everything you ever wanted to know (and possibly a few things you *never* wanted to know) about the human body. You'll also learn about the importance of leading a healthy lifestyle, eating healthy food, getting lots of exercise and getting an education.

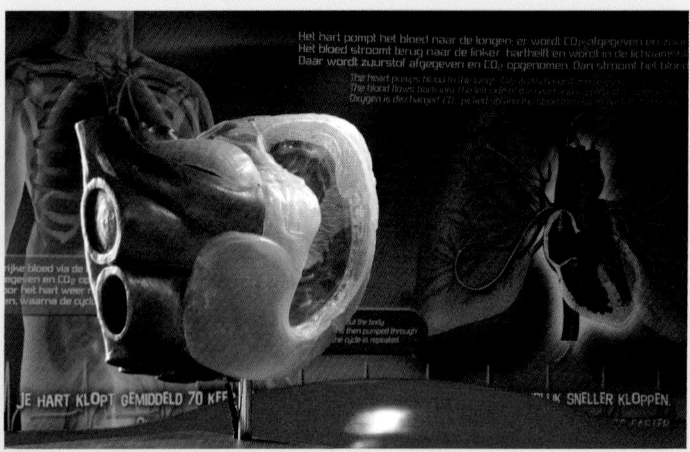

cool, yEaH?

Almost half of the 206 bones in your body are in your hands and feet, but babies actually have 300 bones at birth (although no knee-caps)!

Some weird stuff you didn't know about your body: your middle finger is the most sensitive one; you can't sneeze with your eyes open; if you chew gum when you cut onions, you won't cry. Try it yourself if you don't believe us!

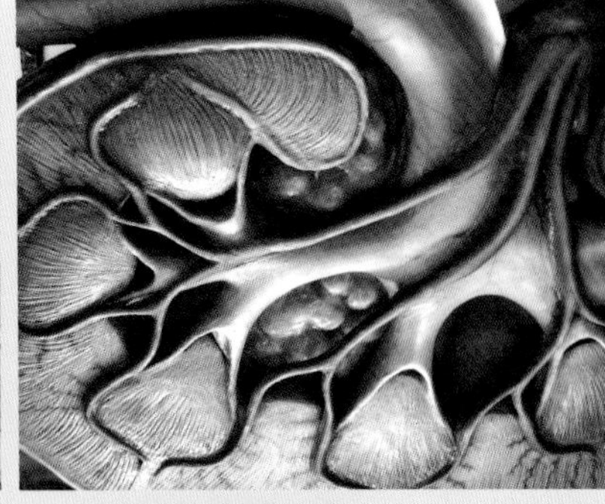

cool, yEaH?

Efteling has its own radio station that's available on its website. The station broadcasts cheery music, Efteling and general news and fairy tales for kids.

It is the most popular amusement park in the Netherlands, and in Europe only Disneyland Paris has more visitors.

a Real fairy tale forest

You've probably heard of the Brothers Grimm, Hans Christian Andersen and Charles Perrault. They're some of the most famous fairy tale authors in the world. The Brothers Grimm wrote tales such as *Snow White*, *Hansel and Gretel*, *Rumpelstiltskin* and *Rapunzel*; Hans Christian Andersen wrote *The Little Mermaid*, *Thumbelina* and *The Ugly Duckling*; and Charles Perrault wrote *Cinderella*, *Sleeping Beauty*, *Little Red Riding Hood* and *Puss in Boots*. Maybe you've also heard of *1001 Nights*, stories which date back to the 9th century.

The Efteling amusement park is all about fairy tales, and the most famous of them are recreated in the Fairy Tale Forest. Over the years, amusement rides, such as a haunted house, roller coasters and water rides have been added. Efteling is divided into three sections: the theme park, the hotel and a golf course. The park doesn't feel like a typical amusement park, though. It has been built in a dense forest, with large ponds and flower gardens. The theatre stages musicals based on fairy tales, such as *Sleeping Beauty* and *The Little Mermaid*. You'll love spending the day here, and it's totally worth the one-hour drive to Tilburg!

THE ORIGINAL HARLEM!

Haarlem is an area in North Holland where the Counts of Holland lived and ruled between the 10th and 16th centuries. During the Golden Age, the city prospered, with linen and silk trading, beer brewing, and tulip growing. Tulip bulb-growing continues there to this day, which is why the town is nicknamed: Bloemenstad (flower city). It is the main flower-growing district in Holland and a major producer of flower bulbs for export.

Haarlem revolves around De Grote Markt, the city's main square, where a huge street market still takes place. This square and the surrounding streets look typically Dutch, with tiny, leaning houses, laddered roofs and quaint little shops. This historic city also has the oldest museum in the country, the Teylers Museum, which brings together science, technology and Dutch art. Besides, the Zandvoort sand dunes are nearby, so make a day of it and stop by before heading out to the beach and tanning under the Dutch sun (SEE PAGE 128)!

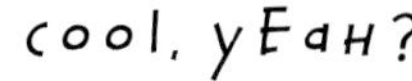

Harlem in New York City was founded by a Dutchman called Peter Stuyvesant. Originally it was named Nieuw Haarlem (New Haarlem).

The town of Haarlem was given the right to include the Count's sword and cross in its coat of arms after capturing the city of Damietta (in today's Egypt) during the 5th Crusade.

a NatuRal adventuRE

De Hoge Veluwe National Park was started by a wealthy couple, Anton Kröller and Helene Kröller-Müller. He was a hunter, and she was an art collector. So it's not surprising that they came up with a way to bring nature and culture together! They bought the property, put up a fence, brought in animals, built the hunting lodge and started to build a museum. But it was an expensive endevour, and it soon became clear that they couldn't keep up the property. Eventually, it was donated to the state. The park is unique, with woods, ridges, lakes, hills and drift sand. You'll often see red deer, mouflon, roe deer and wild boar. You can even visit some underground animals in the Museonder—an underground museum.

As for culture, the Kröller Müller Museum displays the couple's art collection, which includes many works by Vincent van Gogh, Georges Seaurat and Pablo Picasso. The museum's sculpture garden also contains works by several artists, including Auguste Rodin and Henry Moore. The old lodge is now a museum, too, and is named after St. Hubert, the patron saint of hunters. The park is huge, and there's no way to walk through it all—not in a few hours, anyway. Grab a white bicycle at the entrance (they're free to use!) and start your natural and cultural adventure. And to really connect with nature, why not 'go Dutch', set up camp in the park's campsite and spend the night!?

JUNIOR FAR AWAY JETSETTERS

cool, yEaH?

The park has 1,700 white bicycles and 40 km (25 miles) of cycle paths.

Helene Kröller-Müller was one of the first art collectors to pay attention to the works of Vincent van Gogh. Not many women at the time were art collectors, let alone with that kind of buying power.

an ancient town by the sea

Hoorn is a coastal city in North Holland. Its city centre is ancient, with over 300 monumental buildings, and lots of small boutiques selling all sorts of cool and interesting stuff you won't find anywhere else. There's also a poster museum and a toy museum! But, deep down inside, Hoorn is still a quaint fishing town. You can feel it as you walk around the old harbour. During the Golden Age, the Dutch East India Company used Hoorn's harbour as a base for its trade. The company's fleet of ships would arrive, bringing precious cargo from the Far East. Spices like pepper, nutmeg, cloves and mace were popular and made a lot of money for the company. It's hard to imagine, but the spices that your mom and dad ordinarily use when they're cooking today were almost as valuable as gold back then.

Eventually, as trading decreased, so did the use of the port of Hoorn. The town resumed fishing, only to stop again during French rule by Napoléon. At that time, the sea was no longer the city's focus, and Hoorn gradually became a market for agricultural products for Friesland (West Frisia). With the arrival of the railway, those products were sent farther. Later, the construction of the Afsluitdijk (see page 106) closed off the IJmeer and meant that Hoorn's seaport was virtually unused for trade. It soon became a seaport and a popular recreation and water sports harbour.

cool, yEaH?

Cape Horn in South America was named by a Dutch explorer from Hoorn to honour his hometown.

Hoorn is one of the most historic cities in the Netherlands, and you can get totally into it by touring the region on steam train!

cool, yEaH?

Keukenhof is one of Holland's 'official visit rooms' and has been visited by lots of famous people, like US President Eisenhower, US President Clinton and Queen Elizabeth II of England. Queen Beatrix is quite often their host, and they all dress their best to come here!

The unforgettable display of flowers is created by more than seven million tulips, daffodils, hyacinths, spring bulbs and hundreds of trees.

NOW THIS IS FLOWER POWER

A few hundred years ago, the area around Keukenhof was used for hunting and herb collecting. The herbs were used in the kitchen of the nearby castle. This is how the name Keukenhof came to be (*keuken* = kitchen, *hof* = garden). Over the years, several rich families have owned the property. One family hired the designers of Vondelpark (SEE PAGE 68) to design an English-style garden around the castle.

In 1949, the mayor of Lisse (the closest town) and several flower bulb growers and exporters got together to organize an outdoor flower exhibition. The goal was for growers from all over the Netherlands and Europe to show off their flowers. Since that time, the exhibition has blossomed into the largest flower garden in the world. It's only open in spring, from the time tulips bloom until they die, but this festival of colour is definitely worth the wait. A great way to make your way through the garden is by whisper boat. But if you're full of energy, head over to the large playground with jungle gyms, an animal paddock, a maze and a giant chessboard! And don't forget to check some of the 150 sculptures in the museum. But, most importantly, don't forget your camera... or you'll really regret it!

a sandy, sunny seaside resort

Not far from Amsterdam is a city called The Hague. Even though Amsterdam is the country's capital, it's here that the government of the Netherlands sits. This has many reasons, but partly because, at one time, Belgium and the Netherlands were one country, with the capital moving between Brussels and Amsterdam. The government was in The Hague because it was in-between. Once the countries split, the two cities remained the respective capitals, and the new Dutch-only government stayed in The Hague. The Hague is on the North Sea coast of Holland, and is made up of eight districts, one of which is the beach resort of Scheveningen. The area dates back to around 1280, when Anglo Saxons or Vikings lived there. Fishing was the main industry in the village for a long time. But, as Scheveningen grew, people realized that being on the coast made it vulnerable to storms and attacks by enemy fleets, and eventually a protected harbour was built. In 1818 a wooden building was constructed on a dune, and this was the beginning of the use of Scheveningen as a seafront resort. In 1886, a time when a lot of Europeans were

cool, yeah?

At age 14, Crown Princess Beatrix (now Queen Beatrix) was made the mayor of Madurodam (a miniature city!). She remained mayor until she was crowned Queen of the Netherlands.

The Hague gets its name from 'Des Graven Hage', which means 'the count's woods', suggesting the area was once the local Count's private property.

starting to go on holiday abroad, the magnificent hotel and restaurant Kurhaus opened, bringing hundreds of wealthy tourists from around Europe to frolic on the beach or gamble in the casino. Today the area's boardwalk over the long sandy beaches, the beautiful double-decker pier and the lighthouse make it a favourite getaway. You'll see people windsurfing, sailing, kite surfing, fishing, scuba diving, and even riding horse buggies on the wet sand. But even if you're not into hanging out at the beach, there are tons of things to do! Visit the museum Beelden aan Zee to see sculptures (there's also a sand sculptures competition every summer); take a tour on a navy ship to learn about everyday life on a boat; check out Madurodam, a miniature city with all of the Netherlands' famous features; visit the Sea Life centre to learn about the marine world; and be especially sure not to miss Panorama Mesdag—a large, cylindrical painting of what the area looked like in 1881. It's so life-like, you'll feel like you're standing on a high sand dune, overlooking the sea, the beaches and the village back in the day.

Rail back in time

Because the Netherlands has so many rivers and canals, travelling by boat has always made sense. This explains, in part, why the Netherlands was slower to start using trains than most other countries. But once railways were introduced in the 1830s, they quickly became popular with passengers. They were faster than using the waterways (not to mention more exciting, back in the time!). Freight continued to be shipped by water, while passengers went by train. By 1900, a complete national network had been built. Unfortunately, during World War II most of the railways were destroyed and had to be rebuilt from scratch.

The Dutch Railway Museum was opened in 1927 in the city of Utrecht, not far from Amsterdam, in the old Maliebaan railway station. It's got dozens of old trains, carriages, control towers, paintings and railway objects spanning the whole 20th century. The station has been completely renovated and restored to look like it did in 1874. If you think this is just another railway museum, you're sorely mistaken: this is the railway museum, and it's all thought out for kids like you, so you'll never want to leave.

The coolest areas are the 'lands', each showcasing a different theme related to trains. For example, Dream Journeys takes you right into a busy station in the times of the Orient Express (a very fancy train that used to travel between Paris and Istanbul around the late 19th century). In Steel Monsters you'll get to see some of the largest and most powerful trains ever used in the Netherlands. And in the Workshop you'll discover the inner workings of trains and what it takes to maintain and operate a railway network. Before you go, definitely don't forget to try the rides outdoors! During the last weekend of the month, you can also hop aboard the Reminiscence Express, an antique train that will take you to some of the most scenic areas of Utrecht!

SpooRwEgMusEum - thE dutch Railway MusEum
Het Spoorwegmuseum (Utrecht)

REALLY COOL!
JETSETTERS

cool, yEaH?

The museum's collection was once located in Amsterdam's Rijksmuseum.

The Arend, the first steam locomotive in the Netherlands, is on display outside The Great Discovery.

TEXEL GETS A 'SEAL' OF APPROVAL

Texel is an island in North Holland, in a province called Friesland. There have been small villages on the island since the 13th century, but it was during the Golden Age that it became busier. Many of the Dutch East India Company ships (SEE PAGE 14) left from Texel and, with so many people around, it's unsurprising that it developed quickly. Today it is again low-key, and famous for its large beach, quaint villages and amazing nature reserves. The beach runs along the entire west coast on the North Sea shores, so be warned that the water is sort of cold most of the time. Texel is also famous for the Wadden Sea flats, in the small body of water between the island, North Holland and the Afsluitdijk (SEE PAGE 106). The way the tide comes in turns parts of it into sandbanks in low tide, so you can actually walk on the sea bed at times! However, you should never go far without a local guide, as high tides can surprise you when you're far from the beach.

There are several quaint villages on the island, but the most interesting village is De Koog, a favourite seaside resort. It's there that you'll find Ecomare, a museum about sea life, packed with exhibits and a sea aquarium. The highlights are the bird and seal sanctuaries sheltering sick, wounded and abandoned animals, including the victims of oil spills. Young ducks are the most common 'customers' of the bird sanctuary, where they are taken care of and released into the wild in spring. In the seal sanctuary, some 30 seals in need are cared for every year. After recovery, they're released in the shallow Wadden Sea. Seals are fed at 11 am and 3 pm!

Texel's amazing dune park is another thing you won't want to miss. It's only accessible through Ecomare, so make sure you go on one of the marked trails when you visit (1-3 km). And don't forget your camera, your bird-watching binoculars and, most importantly, your windbreaker and umbrella, since the weather in Friesland can be temperamental!

cool, yEaH?

The 'x' in the name is actually pronounced 'ss'.

If you like what you see in Ecomare, you can become a 'friend' and help rescue birds and seals in need of support. Spread the word!

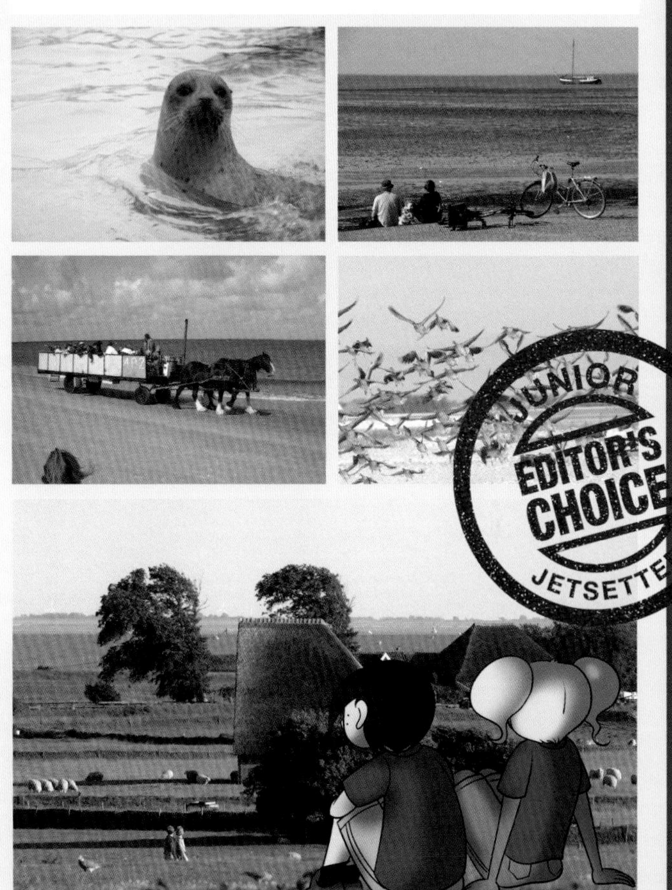

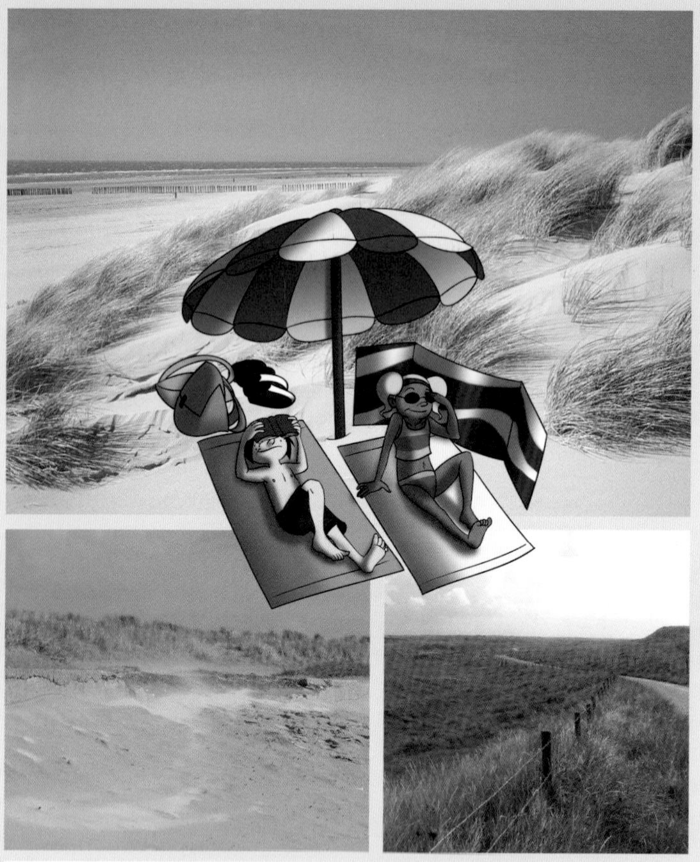

cool, yEaH?

When fishing stopped being the main industry, Zandvoorters grew potatoes in the sand dunes. They were some of the toughest in the world, not susceptible to any potato diseases!

Zandvoort's coat of arms has three golden fish that signify its history as a fishing village.

spend a day in the dunes

Zandvoort is an old fishing village in North Holland, half an hour from Amsterdam by train. Like Scheveningen (see page 122), it's a major beach resort, famous for its beautiful sand dunes—a protected natural site. You can walk on a path through the dunes for hours, but don't touch any plants and leave nothing behind but your footprints! The 9-kilometre beach offers many watersports—all you need to enjoy a sunny Dutch day. It wasn't until the early 20th century that tourism became the main industry in the area, helped by the construction of a railway connection and the opening of hotels, shops, cafés and restaurants. For hundreds of years, fishing was the main industry in Zandvoort. But during the French rule of Napoléon Bonaparte, fishing almost completely stopped. First, the French did not allow the fishermen to set out for sea. And second, France was at war with England, just across the sea.

Once you're in the area, take a look at nearby IJmuiden, just north of Zandvoort. IJmuiden means 'the mouth of the IJ,' because it's at the end of the North Sea Canal. The canal was dug in the 1870s, after the damming of the Zuidersee, to connect Amsterdam's harbours to the open sea (see pages 106 and 130). It links to the IJ in Amsterdam, then through to the Rhine Canal, the Danube River and other major waterways in Europe!

COME AND SEE WHERE THE ZUIDERZEE USED TO BE!

Thousands of years ago, in the spot where the Zuiderzee Museum stands, there was a lake. Over centuries, the shores eroded until the lake opened into the North Sea. North Sea waters quickly flooded the area, creating the salty Zuiderzee. Although this sounds disastrous, something good came out of it: ships were able to sail out to sea. Fishing villages popped up and soon towns developed. Fishermen were able to trade with neighbouring countries, and the Dutch empire grew. The construction of a huge dam called the Afsluitdijk (SEE PAGE 106) was the end of the Zuiderzee. The shallow salt water that resulted became the IJsselmeer, a fresh water lake.

The Zuiderzeemuseum was opened to preserve the history of this important body of water and the communities that surrounded its shores. The exhibits are mostly about the history of the area before the dam was built. You can also visit The Ship's Hall, which holds a collection of old ships. Climb up to look at them from above, then head down to walk around them.

But it's Museum Park, outside, that you won't want to miss. It recreates a 19th century Dutch settlement with a harbour, a church neighbourhood, a town canal, a fishing village and a nature area. And it feels quite real!

COOL, YEAH?

The IJsselmeer is the largest lake in Western Europe.

In Museum Park's chapel, you can sometimes watch an old-fashioned church wedding take place!

Zuiderzee Museum: Land of Water

Het Zuiderzeemuseum: Land of Water (Enkhuizen)

AFC Ajax's Amsterdam ArenA
Arena Boulevard 29, Zuidoost (Nl). +31 (0)203111444. Tours: +31 (0)203111336, www.ajax.nl, www.amsterdamarena.nl. Museum Hours: Seasonal: Apr-Sept: Mon-Fri: 9:30am-6pm, Sat-Sun 10am-5pm. Closed on Sundays, when Ajax plays at home. Tours: Mon-Fri, last Sun of month 11am, 12:30pm, 2:30pm, 4:30pm. Sat & holidays: 11am, 12:15pm, 1:30pm, 2:45pm, 4:30pm. Different tours times in the off season. Please consult the website. Museum: Adults €3,50, Children €3,50 Tours: Adults €9, Children (5-12) €8 Photo: €6 (2 for €10). Metro 54 to Gein (stopping at Strandvliet, Bijlmer and Duivendrecht) links Amsterdam Arena to the centre of Amsterdam.
Alkmaar Cheese Market
Waagplein, Alkmaar. www.kaasmarkt.nl. Hours: Apr-Aug: Fri 10am-12:30pm. Tickets for the Cheese Market for children (5-12): € 4,50, available by VVV Alkmaar. They can experience the market at close distance: an enclosed part of the market is accessible for children who visit the cheese market. Dates/ time change yearly, please check website for info. Presentation given in Dutch, German, English, French. **Dutch Cheese Museum – Hollands Kaasmuseum** Waagplein 2. Tel + 31 (0)725155516. www.kaasmuseum.nl. Hours: Apr-Oct & Christmas: Mon-Sat 10am-4pm (Fri from 9am). Adults €3,00, Children (under 12) €1,50, Children (under 4) Free. For more information check www.vvvalkmaar.nl, or contact by email info@vvvalkmaar.nl, or phone +31 (0)725114284. **NOTE:** Other cheese markets in Edam, Hoorn, Gouda and Woerden. Woerden is the only production cheese market in the Netherlands.
Amsterdam Walks
Suggested Itineraries and information about itineraries:
http://www.amsterdamtourist.nl/en/visiting/spotlight/walking
http://www.amsterdamtourist.nl/en/visiting/practicalinformation/products/walkingtours - http://www.amsterdam.info/itineraries/historic/
Allard Pierson Museum
Dept. of the University of Amsterdam. Oude Turfmarkt 127. Tel. + 31 (0)205252556, www.allardpiersonmuseum.nl. Hours: Tues-Fri 10am-5pm, Sat-Sun 1pm-5pm. Adults €5, Seniors €2,50, Children (4-16) €2,50, Children (< 4) Free. Trams 4, 9, 16, 24, 25 to Rokin.
Amsterdam Historical Museum (Amsterdams Historisch M.)
Two entrances: Nieuwezijds Voorburgwal 357. Or Kalverstraat 92. Tel +31(0)20 523 1822, www.ahm.nl. Hours: Mon-Fri 10am-5pm, Sat-Sun 11am-5pm. Adults €8, Seniors €6, Children (6-18) €4, Children (5 and under) Free. Tram 1, 2, 5 to Spui & 4, 9, 14, 16, 24, 25 to Rokin. Audio tours and children exhibits/activities available.
Amsterdam Roots Festival
www.amsterdamroots.nl. Check website for yearly details.
Anne Frank House – Anne Frankhuis
Prinsengracht 267. Tel +31 (0)205567100, www.annefrank.org. Hours: Mar-Sept: Sun-Fri 9am-9pm, Sat 9am-10pm. July-Aug: Daily 9am-10pm. Sept-Mar: Daily 9am-7pm. Adults €8,50, Children (10-17) €4, Children (9 and under) Free. Audio tours available. Advance tickets strongly advised, esp. in summer months (long queues). Fabulous store with educational materials at the exit. Buy your own copy of Anne Frank's Diary on site.
BIKING IN AMSTERDAM
Damstraat Rent-A-Bike
Damstraat 20 - 22. Tel +31 (0)206255029, www.bikes.nl.
MacBike
Stationsplein 12. Tel +31 (0)206200985, www.macbike.nl. Rentals of bikes,

kids' wagons and kids seats, transporter bikes, tandem bikes, also tours.

Mike's Bike Tours

Kerkstraat 134. Tel +31 (0)206227970. www.mikesbikeamsterdam.com. Hours: Mar-Nov 9am-6pm, Dec-Feb 10am-6pm. Offers tours and bike rentals. Bikes of all sizes, colours, decorations and designs are available. Tours in/ outside Amsterdam vary in level of difficulty.

StarBikes

De Ruyterkade 105. Behind Central Station. Tel +31(0)203308132, www.StarBikesRental.com.

Yellow Bike

Nieuwezijds Kolk 29. Tel +31 (0)206206940, www.yellowbike.nl

Corpus Experience

Willem Einthovenstraat 1. Oegstgeest. Tel +31 (0)717510200 www. corpusexperience.nl. Hours: Jan-Jun: Tues-Sun 9:30am-5pm (Thurs until 8pm). Oct-Dec: Tues-Sun 9:30am-5pm (Thurs until 8pm). Adults €16,50, Children (8-14) €14. Journey starts every 7 minutes. Be advised that children under 8 cannot enter Corpus.

Eastindiaman Amsterdam

Oosterdok 2. Tel +31 (0)205232222, www.scheepvaartmuseum.nl. Hours: Tues-Sun 10am-5pm. Adults €5, Seniors €5, Children (4 and over) €5, Children (0-3) Free. Docked in front of NEMO. Ship will be moved to the Maritime Museum's dock when it reopens (check website for updates). Also open in Mon. in June, July and August.

Efteling Park

Europalaan 1, Kaatsheuvel. Tel +31 (0)416288111, www.efteling.nl. Hours: Seasonal; check website for specific opening times. Apr-Oct: Daily 10am-6pm. July-Aug: Sun-Fri 10am-9pm, Sat 10am-midnight. Take the train to ´s-Hertogenbosch, from here there are bustransfers to Efteling. If driving, follow general directions to Tilburg. Adults €27, Seniors €25, Children (under 4) Free, Two-day ticket €49. July-Aug: Adults €29, Seniors €27.

FLEA MARKETS

Albert Cuyp Market

Bustling market in canalside. The largest, cheapest in Amsterdam, and one of the oldest (100 years old). Specialties: (cheap) flowers, fruits, vegetables, fish, meats, spices, chocolate, cheese, flowers and plants to clothes, jewelry, shoes, bike accessories. Location: Albert Cuypstraat (De Pijp neighbourhood). Tram: 3, 4, 12, 16 and 24. Open: all year, Mon - Sat 9 a.m. - 5 p.m.

Antiekmarkt De Looier

Antiques and curiosa market - one of the few covered markets in Amsterdam. Specialty: furniture, jewelry, silverware, collectables. Located: Elandsgracht 109, 1016 TT. Tram: Elandsgracht: tram 7, 10, 17 & 20. Open: each day of the week except Friday: 11am -5pm. Friday closed.

Art Plein Spui

www.artplein-spui.nl. Art market where artist sell their own originals. Speciality: Original prints, small oil paintings. Located: Spui Plein, 1012 WZ. Tram: 1,2, 4, 5, 9, 16, 17, 24 and 25 – tram stop Spui. Open: Sunday 10 a.m. – 5 p.m. (not in winter).

Boekenmarkt

www.deboekenmarktophetspui.nl. Very popular book market. Speciality: Books, cards, maps, engravings. Located: Oudemanhuispoort. Tram: Muntplein: tram 4, 9, 14, 16, 24 & 25. Open: Monday - Saturday 10.00 am - 4.00 pm

Farmer's Market, Nieuwmarkt - Boerenmarkt
Location: Nieuwmarkt (in the Old City Center). Open: Year-round, Saturdays 9 a.m. - 5 p.m. Metro: Nieuwmarkt. Popular farmers' market with mostly organic food. Near De Waag, Chinatown and the Redlight District. Central, less busy (and smaller) than Noordermarkt.

Farmer's Market, Noordermarkt - Boerenmarkt
(Biological Fresh Food Market - Biologische versmarkt)
Biological food, fresh fruits, cheese and cakes, snacks. The most popular Amsterdam market at the moment. Speciality: Mushrooms, biological food, cheese, fresh fish, herbs. Located: Noordermarkt, 1015 MV. Tram: Westermarkt -tram 13 & 17 or Marnixbad - tram 3 & 10. Open: Saturday 9.00 am - 3.00 pm.

Postzegelmarkt
A collector's market. Specialty: Stamps, coins, old postcards, commemorative medals. Located: Nieuwezijds Voorburgwal 280, 1012 RL. Tram: station Het Spui - tram 1, 2, 5, 13, 17 & 20. Open: Wednesday & Saturday 10 a.m. – 4 p.m.

Waterlooplein Flea Market
Flea market, an unique 300-stall outdoor bazaar is full of curiosa, general bric-a-brac, second-hand clothing, CDs, DVDs, appliances and other brand new and used goods. Speciality: Second-hand clothes, curiosa. Located: Waterlooplein, 1011 PG. Tram: 1, 2, 5, 13 from Magna Plaza or 14 from Central Station. Open: Monday - Friday 9.00 am - 5.30 pm; Saturday: 8.30 am –5.30 pm.

Flower Market – Bloemenmarkt
Singel between Koningsplein and Muntplein. Hours: Mon-Sat 9am-5:30pm, Sun 11am-5:30pm. Tram: any passing Rokin and Muntplein.

Gassan Diamonds
Nieuwe Uilenburgerstraat 173-175. Tel +31(0)206225333. www.gassandiamonds.com. Hours: Mon-Fri 9am-5pm. Free Adm.

Grachtenfestival
www.grachtenfestival.nl. Locations and times vary. Check website.

GVB
Museum: Haarlemmermeerstation. Amstelveenseweg 264. Tel +31 (0)206737538, www.museumtramlijn.org. Hours: Mar-Oct: Sun 11am-5:30pm. Seasonal – check website for hours. For general info, maps and tour information, visit GVB kiosk outside Centraal Station.

Haarlem (Tourism)
Zijlsingel 1, +31 (0) 235115115, www.haarlem.nl, www.vvvhaarlem.nl

Hoge Veluwe National Park
www.hogeveluwe.nl. Hours: Seasonal. 9am-6pm or longer. Check website for times. Park only: Adults €7, Children (6-12) €3,50, Children (under 6) Free. Visitors' Centre, museum and residence have different hours. Check website. Residence is only open with a guided tour. Additional fees apply for residence and museum. **Kröller-Müller Museum**, www.kmm.nl, Tel + 31 (0) 318591241.

Harbour Walks
www.easterndocklands.com. Several suggested walking and cycling tours are listed on the website.

Hermitage Museum Amsterdam
Nieuwe Herengracht 14. Tel +31 (0)205308755, www.hermitage.nl. Hours: Daily 10am-5pm. Adults €8, Children (under 16) Free.

Hoorn (Tourism)
Stadhuis, Nieuwe Steen 1. Tel +31 (0)229252040, www.hoorn.nl.
Veemarkt 4. Tel +31 (0)72 511 4284, www.vvvhoorn.nl.
See also www.hoorngids.nl for more information.

Hortus Botanicus Amsterdam – Amsterdam Botanical Garden
Plantage Middenlaan 2a. Tel +31 (0)20 625 9021, www.hortus-botanicus.nl. Hours: Mon-Fri 9am-5pm, Sat-Sun 10am-5pm. Adults €7, Seniors €3,50, Children (5-14) €3,50. Tram 9, 14 to Mr. Visserplein. Tram 6 (Mon-Fri) last stop. Metro Waterlooplein (Hortusplantsoen exit). Tours available every Sunday at 2pm (€1).

Iamsterdam
www.iamsterdam.com. For tourist information visit the official kiosks in Centraal Station, Museumplein. Street staff identified by red uniforms with logo.

Jewish Historical Museum – Joods Historisch Museum
Nieuwe Amstelstraat 1. Tel +31 (0)205310310, www.jhm.nl. Hours: Daily 11am-5pm. Adults €7,50, Seniors €4,50, Children (13-17) €3, Children (under 13) Free. Metro 51, 53, 54 to Waterlooplei. Tram 9, 14 to Waterlooplein. Activities for kids available, advance booking needed. All take place in the Joods for kids. Visit cafe downstairs!!!

Keukenhof Tulip Park
Stationsweg 166a, Lisse. Tel +31 (0)252465555, www.keukenhof.nl. Hours: Mar-May: Daily 8am-7:30pm. Adults €13,50, Seniors €13, Children (4-11) €6,50. Combined bus and entrance ticket is valid on all direct Connexxion routes to Keukenhof. Travellers with a Combi-ticket from Amsterdam can switch to Keukenhof shuttle bus at Schiphol (no. 58). Nature determines when bulbs bloom. If cold, it will take longer. Check website for opening dates. Free guided tours available daily 11am and 2pm. Boat tour €7,50 extra per person.

Madame Tussauds
Dam 20. Tel +31 (0)205230623, www.madametussauds.nl. Hours: Daily 10am-5:30pm. Adults €21, Children (5-15) €16, Children (under 5) Free. Family rates also available.

Museum Van Loon
Keizersgracht 672. Tel (0)206245255, www.museumvanloon.nl. Hours: Wed-Mon 11am-5pm. Adults €6, Children (6-18) €4, Children (under 6) Free. Trams 16, 24, 25 to Keizersgracht. Guided tours are available for €48 + €4 per person. Outside regular hours, tours are €58. Reservations are required.

Museum Willet-Holthuysen
Herengracht 605. Tel +31(0)205231822, www.willetholthuysen.nl. Hours: Mon-Fri 10am-5pm, Sat-Sun 11am-5pm. Adults €6, Seniors €4,50, Children (6-18) €3, Children (under 6) Free. Tram 4, 9, 14 to Rembrandtplein. Metro Waterlooplein.

Natura Artis Magistra
Plantage Kerklaan 38-40. Tel +31 (0)205233400, www.artis.nl. Hours: Daily 9am-5pm (6pm in summer). Adults €17,70, Seniors €16,50, Children (3-9) €14,50. Guided tours in English available every Sunday at 11am. Ticket provides admission to the Planetarium, Geological Museum, Aquarium and Zoological Museum. Tram 6, 9, 14 or 'Artis Expres' (shuttle boat).

Nieuwe Kerk – New Church
Dam Square. Tel +31 (0)206386909, www.nieuwekerk.nl. Hours: Daily 10am-6pm (Thurs until 10pm). Adults €10, Children (6-15) €7,50, Children (5 and under) Free. Guided tours (in several languages) are available but should be

requested in advance. Get permission at front desk if you want to take pictures inside.

Oude Kerk – Old Church

Oudekerksplein (ingang zuidzijde) 23. Tel +31 (0)206258284. Hours: Church Mon-Sat 11am-5pm, Sun 1pm-5pm. Adults €5, Seniors €4, Children (under 12) Free. Tower: Sat-Sun 1pm-5pm (every half hour). Adults €5, Children €5. Tram 4, 9, 16, 24, 25. Check the Oude Kerk's excellent website, which includes a database of all inventoried graves out of the 10,000 people buried in the church. Computers also available on site for public use.

Our Lord in the Attic – Ons' Lieve Heer op Solder

Oudezijds Voorburgwal 40. Tel +31(0)206246604, www.opsolder.nl. Hours: Mon-Sat 10am-5pm, Sun 1pm-5pm. Adults €7, Children (5-18) €1. Metro Nieuwmarkt. Trams 4, 9, 16, 24, 25 to Dam Square (5 minute walk).

Pathé Tuschinski Cinema

Reguliersbreestraat 26-34 (just steps away from Rembrandtplein. www.tuschinski.nl (check website for movie times). Private cabins available.

Portuguese Synagogue - Esnoga

Mr. Visserplein 3. Tel +31 (0)206245351. www.esnoga.com. Hours: Apr-Oct: Sun-Fri 10am-4pm. Nov-Mar: Sun-Fri 10am-4pm (Fri until 2pm).Adults €6,50, Seniors €5, Children (10-17) €4. Metro: 51, 53 and 54. Tram 9,14 to Waterlooplein. Security features in place, ring bell to gain access. This is a working synagogue, please show respect. Men will be requested to wear a *yamukah* on their heads.

Rembrandt House Museum – Museum het Rembrandthuis

Jodenbreestraat 4. Tel +31 (0)205200400, www.rembrandthuis.nl. Hours: Daily 10am-5pm. Adults €8, Children (6-15) €1,50, Children (under 6) Free. Admission includes audioguide. Tram Lines 9,14 to Waterlooplein. Metro - Every line from and to CS Amsterdam to Nieuwmarkt (Hoogstraat exit). Check out the interactive section of the website for kids' activities (booked in advance). Etching demonstrations available every day, the paint preparation demonstrations are available on weekends – both are free.

Rijksmuseum

Jan Luijkenstraat 1. Tel +31 (0)206747000, www.rijksmuseum.nl. Hours: Daily 9am-6pm (Frid until 8:30pm). Adults €10, Children (18 and under) Free. Tram 2, 5 to Hobbemastraat, 12 to Concertgebouw Metro Weesperplein then tram 6, 7, 10 to Spiegelgracht. Taking pictures is not allowed in the museum. 'Gordon the Warden' (guide and activity book for kids 6-12): Join Gordon the Warden in looking for five of the Rijksmuseum's masterpieces. This search leads you to a model ship, a doll's house, two portraits of powerful Amsterdam citizens, a fine mess by Jan Steen and Rembrandt's The Night Watch. The Gordon the Warden search can be purchased from the Information Desk for €1 a piece. Please note that the Rijkmuseum is undergoing profound renovation work. Most of the building is closed, only a sample of Golden Age masterpieces are visitable at this point. Check website for updates on opening date of renovated wings.

Scheveningen, The Hague (Tourism)

Gevers Deynootweg 1134. Tel +31 (0)9003403505, www.scheveningen.nl. The Hague Greeters, local residents, will guide you through the city - check the website for details on this service. See also www.scheveningen.info.

science center NEMO

Oosterdok 2 (turn left outside Amsterdam Centraal Station, follow New Amsterdam route, past Chinese floating restaurant and harbour bridge. Tel

+ 31 (0)205313233, www.e-nemo.nl. Hours: Tues-Sun 10am-5pm. Adults €11,50, Children €11,50. Bus 22, 42, 43 to Kadijksplein. Children under 12 require an adult to conduct experiments in the Wonder Lab. Please note that NEMO's activities are divided by age group. There are also 'Peep Show' cabins about sexuality, geared at kids 12 and up. Admission only when authorized by guardians (who are NOT allowed in). Shows are age-appropriate.

Spoorwegmuseum

Maliebaanstation, Utrecht (near main street). Tel +31(0)302306206, www.spoorwegmuseum.nl. Hours: Tues-Sun 10am-5pm (Mondays during school holidays). Adults €14,50, Seniors €13, Children (3-12) €11,50, Children (under 3) Free. A special shuttle train runs daily between Utrecht CS and the Railway Museum. From Utrecht CS, take most bus lines on main street.

St. Nicolaaskerk

Prins Hendrikkade 73. www.muziekindenicolaas.nl. Check website for concert and evensong times.

Stedelijk Museum

Museumplein. Tel +31 (0)205732911, www.stedelijk.nl. Check website for current exhibitions and hours. Sundays will be family days at the New Stedelijk. Audio tours available. Spend the day with the artists (Sundays). The Stedelijk Museum has been undergoing renovation and expansion work in Museumplein. Temporary exhbitions in other venues in Amsterdam. Check website for info and update on opening schedule of the new building.

Texel Island (Tourism)

Emmalaan 66, Den Burg, +31 (0)222 314 741, www.vvvtexel.nl. Travel to the island can easily be done by train northwards to Den Helder and then with the Royal TESO ferry. Check the ferry or VVV websites for appropriate seasonal links. **Ecomare:** Ruijslaan 92, 1796 AZ De Koog, Texel. Tel +31-(0)222317741, www.exomare.nl. Hours: Daily 9am-5pm. Adults €8,50, Children (4-13) €5,50, Children (under 4) Free. **Maritiem & Jutters Museum:** Barentszstraat 21, 1792 AD Oudeschild. Tel (0)22314956. Tues-Sat 10am-5pm, Sun 12noon-5pm. Adults €5,50, Children (under 14) €4.

Tropenmuseum – Tropics Museum

Linnaeusstraat 2. Tel +31 (0)205688200, www.tropenmuseum.nl. Hours: Daily 10am-5pm. Adults €8, Children (6-17) €4, Children (under 6) Free. Tram 3, 7, 9, 10, 14 and bus 22. The available programs are in Dutch only. However, the museum is very well structured, and is visually very easy to follow for both parents and kids. Audio tour and guidebook are available in English, and its utilization is advised to enhance the museum interactive elements. Temporary exhibits in the ground floor often tackle issues relevant to kids and/or multiculturalism. **Tropenmuseum Junior** entrance is on the grounfloor (main hall, info desk on the side). Entrance is for kids in a group only (parents: no entry). The exhibitions change every now and then, and are a 2-hour long full sensorial trip to another part of the world. Book/Ask in advance.

Uitmarkt – Outmarket

Tel +31 (0)206211211, www.uitmarkt.nl. Last weekend in August.Free. Check website for location and details. During the festival, look for the International Service Point for more information.

Van Gogh Museum

Museumplein, Paulus Potterstrat 7. Tel +31 (0)205705200, www.vangoghmuseum.nl. Hours: Daily 10am-6pm (Fri until 10pm). Adults €12,50, Youth (13-17) €2,50, Children (under 12) Free. Tram 2, 3, 5, 12 to Van

Baerlestraat, 16, 24 to Museumplein. Bus 145, 170, 172 to Museumplein. Audio tour and guide books for kids (top class!). Workshops by prior booking.

Vondelpark

Friday Night Skate - www.fridaynightskate.com. May-Sept – free children's shows in the open air theatre. Filmmuseum - www.filmmuseum.nl. Performances for children on Wednesday and Sunday afternoons. Check website for complete program.

Westergasfabriek

www.westergasfabriek.nl. Bus 21 to Van Hallstraat. Tram 10 to Van Limburgstirumplein or Van Hallstraat.

Westerkerk

Prinsengracht 281, 1016 GW Amsterdam. Tel +31 (0)206247766. (11am-3pm), www.westerkerk.nl. Apr-Sept: Mon-Fri 11am-3pm
Church Free, Tower €3. Tram 6, 13, 14, 17 to Westermarkt.

Windmill in Sloten

Akersluis 10. +351 (0)26690412, www.molenvansloten.nl. Hours:
Daily 10am-4:30pm. Tram 2 to the last station, cross the park, turn right across the bridge and go straight, crossing the village of Sloten.
You can get there by any means – car, bike, tram, helicopter, boat... English-speaking volunteers are always available in the museum.

Zandvoort aan Zee (Tourism)

Bakkerstraat 2b. Tel +31 (0)235717947, www.zandvoort.nl.

Zuiderzee Museum Land of Water

Wierdijk 12-22, Enkhuizen. Tel +31 (0)228351111, www.zuiderzeemuseum.nl. Daily 10am-5pm. Adults €12,50, Seniors €12,00, Children (4-12) €7,50, Children (3 and under) Free, Family €27,50, Parking €5. Park hours and rates are seasonal. During winter, the park is free.
Museum: train to NS Station Enkhuizen. The Museum is a 10 minute walk from Enkhuizen's NS Station. Follow the signs for 'Zuiderzeemuseum'.
Museum Park: continue past Museum 100 metres. A ferry also runs late March to late October from the NS Station to the park.

BOAT CRUISES

Companies offer different tours – always check website or on-site kiosk.

Canal Company

+351 (0)206239886, www.canal.nl. Canal Bus - day pass €18, Children €12
Pizza Cruise - 1.5 hours, €34,50. Canal Hopper - day pass, Adults €20, Children €15. Canal Bike - 4-seat pedal boats, €7-8/person/hour.

Holland International

+31 (0)206253035, www.hir.nl, 100 Highlights Cruise - 1 hour, Adults €12, Children €6. Ultimate Cruise - 1.5 hours, Adults €17,50, Children €10. Candlelight Cruise - 2 hours, Adults €27,50, Children €17,50. Dinner Cruise - 2.5 hours, Adults €69,50, Children €45

Lovers Boat Company

+31 (0)205305412, www.lovers.nl. Day & Evening Canal Cruises - 1 hour, Adults €11, Children €6. Dinner Cruise - 2 hours, Adults €59, Children €39
Wine & Cheese Candlelight Cruise - 2 hours, €27,50, Children €24,50. Bike & Cruise - (Day Canal Cruise + Yellow Bike tour) - 4 hours, Adults €27,50, Children €14,50. Wax Cruise (cruise & Madame Tussauds) - 2.5 hours, Adults €23,50, Children €16,50. Horror Cruise (cruise & The Amsterdam Dungeon) - 2.5 hours, Adults €23,50, Children €16,50.

Rederij de Nederlanden

+31 (0)204233006, www.denederlanden.com. Cruises & boat rentals.

Water Taxi
+31 (0)205356363, www.water-taxi.nl (boat rental).
De Pannenkoekenboot
+31(0)206368817, www.pannenkoekenboot.nl, 1-hour cruise: Wed, Fri, Sat, Sun 4:30pm-5:30pm & 6pm-7pm. Summer: Wed-Sat, depart 4:30pm & 6pm Adults €14,50, Children (3-12) €9,50. Several different cruises are offered – check website for times and prices. The cruises depart from Amsterdam Noord (as do other cruises in the IJmeer and Haven areas).
BUS TOURS
Most tours, including Hop On-Hop Off Amsterdam and Touristbus Amsterdam are arranged by Tours & Tickets, +31 (0)20 420 4000, www.toursandtickets.nl. Check website for all available tours and schedules.

child-friendly hotel pick

The Bridge Hotel and Apartments
Amstel 107-111, 1018 EM Amsterdam. Tel +31 (0)20.623.7068
Fax +31 (0)20.624.1565 Email: reception@thebridgehotel.nl
www.thebridgehotel.nl. Part of a small local chain of independently run 3-star hotels, The Bridge is a favourite for its location near the Amstel locks. A room with a view will delight your kids. Fourth floor family apartments available for 3 or more nights—our top pick!

recommended house boat and apartment services

Hotels in central Amsterdam can be extremely expensive, especially in high season. When travelling with kids, two alternatives are particularly interesting. One is the rental of serviced apartments, via **www.apartmentservice.com**, starting as low as €130/day, in any part of the city. Even more exciting for kids is the idea of living on a canal boat for some days. You can book guestrooms or a completely private house boat at **www.houseboathotel.nl**. Rooms start at €115, boats (2-5 pax) at around €160/day.

a little dutch: can you say scheepvaartmaatschappij?

Hello / Hi = hallo
Yes / No = ja / nee

Goodbye = tot ziens / dag
Good morning = goedemorgen
Good afternoon = goedemiddag
Good evening = goedenavond
Good night = goedenacht

Please = alstublieft
Thank you (very much) = dank u (wel)
You're welcome (with pleasure) = graag
Excuse me / Sorry = excuseert u mij

HOW TO INTRODUCE YOURSELF

What's your name?
= wat is jouwnaam?
My name is... = mijn naam is...

Pleased to meet you
= aangenaam kennis te maken

How are you?
= hoe gaat het met u?
Fine thanks, and you?
= goed dank u. en met u?

See you later = tot straks

I am American / Canadian / English = ik ben amerikaan/canadees/engels

COMMUNICATING

Do you speak English? = spreekt u Engels?

I speak very little Dutch
= ik spreek weinig Nederlands

I understand = ik begrijp het
I don't understand = ik begrijp het niet

Could you repeat that, please?
= kunt u dat herhalen, alstublieft?

USEFUL LINES AROUND AMSTERDAM

Can you help me? = kunt u me helpen?

I'd like... (something) = ik wil...

What time is it? = hoe laat is het?

How much does this cost? = wat kost dit?

Where is / are... (the toilets)?
= var iz...(het toilet)?

A ticket to... (Central Station), please
= een kaartje naar...
(centraal station), alstublieft

Is this the right way to... ?
=is dit de goede weg naar...?

scheepvaartmaatschappij
= Maritime Society (very useful in Amsterdam...)

spoor
4b
Vertrek 18 22
Intercity
Vertraging ± 20 minuten
Amsterdam Amstel
Voorste treindeel tot
Arnhem
Utrecht C. Veenendaal-de Kl
Ede-Wageningen
Arnhem
Nijmegen

Vertrek 18 37 Intercity
msterdam Amstel
recht Centraal
-Hertogenbosch
ndhoven, Weert
ermond, Sittard
Maastricht/Heerlen

Photograph credits and copyrights (clockwise from top left):

Cover Art: Tapan Gandhi (logo); Maurice Van Tilburg (drawing); Kim Sokol (stamp); A.J. Palmer (font). **Characters:** Kim Sokol. **All stamps:** Kim Sokol.

Front cover endpaper: Amsterdam Tourism & Convention Board in cooperation with Carto Studio BV Amsterdam; courtesy GVB/Metro Amsterdam; courtesy GVB; Gemeente Amsterdam/Stadseel Oud-Zuid. 1: stamp Kim sokol; base photo pfm/jj; 6-10: all pd. 11: pfm/jj. 12-13: pfm/jj. 15: all pfm/jj.17: pfm/jj; pd. 18: base photo pfm/jj; courtesy Science Center NEMO; pfm/jj; courtesy Science Center NEMO; courtesy Science Center NEMO. 20-21: all pfm/jj. 22-23: pfm/jj; Michiel Wijnbergh, courtesy of Van Gogh Museum; pfm/jj; /pd/reproduced by The Yorck Project: 10.000 Meisterwerke der Malerei (2002), Zenodot Verlagsgesellschaft GmbH /gnu-fdl-1.5; butterflies by Mike Hiscott/jj. 24-25: Hasan Sami Bolak /w/gnu-fdl-1.2; courtesy Stadion Amsterdam; /w/pd. 26-27: all pfm/jj. 28-29: all pfm/jj. 30-31: Allard Bovenberg, courtesy Anne Frank Huis Stichting; Allard Bovenberg, courtesy Anne Frank Huis Stichting; Daniel Ullrich /w/gnu-fdl-1.2; courtesy Anne Frank Huis. 32-33: all pfm/jj. 34: all pfm/jj. 36: pfm/jj. 39: all pfm/jj. 40: diamonds all /pd/w/wc; other photos courtesy of Gassan Diamonds. 42-43: all Hans van Heeswijk, courtesy Hermitage Amsterdam. 45: pfm/jj; pfm/jj; pfm/jj; courtesy Hortus Botanicus Amsterdam; courtesy Hortus Botanicus Amsterdam; pfm/jj; pfm/jj; courtesy Hortus Botanicus Amsterdam. 46-47: all pfm/jj. 48-49: all pfm/jj. 50-51: pfm/jj; logo courtesy Artis Natura Magistra; pfm/jj; courtesy Artis Natura Magistra. 52: all courtesy De Nieuwe Kerk Amsterdam. 54: pfm/jj. 56-57: /w/pd; courtesy Amsterdam Municipal Department for the Preservation and Restoration of Historic Buildings and Sites (bMA); pfm/jj; /w/pd; Amsterdam Municipal Department for the Preservation and Restoration of Historic Buildings and Sites (bMA); 58-59: all pfm/jj; ladybugs jj. 60-61: all pfm/jj. 62-63: photo pfm/jj; Rembrandt portrait part of the Rijksmuseum collection /pd; logo courtesy of Museum het Rembrandthuis; pfm/jj; courtesy Museum het Rembrandthuis. 65: Arie de Leeuw, courtesy Rijksmuseum; Jeroen Swolfs, courtesy Rijksmuseum. 66-67: The new Stedelijk Museum, a building designed by Benthem Crouwel Architects, courtesy Stedelijk Museum; pfm/jj; pfm/jj; The new Stedelijk Museum, a building designed by Benthem Crouwel Architects, courtesy Stedelijk Museum. 69: Dirk van der Made w/cc-by-sa-2.5. 71: pfm/jj. 73: Michiel Verbeek /w/gnu-fdl-1.2; pd; pfm/jj. 77: all pfm/jj. 78-79: all pfm/jj. 80-81: all pfm/jj. 83: all pfm/jj. 84: Celesteh /w/cc-by-2.0. 87: pfm/jj. 89: courtesy www.Holland.com. 91: all pfm/jj; ticket courtesy NVB/Nationale Strippen Kaart. 93: courtesy GVB. 95: pfm/jj. 97: pfm/jj. 98-99: all pfm/jj. 100: pfm/jj. 102: pfm/jj. 105: all pfm/jj. 107: pd. 108: Moniek Stap, courtesy VVV Schiereiland Noord-Holland Midden; courtesy VVV Schiereiland Noord-Holland Midden; courtesy VVV Schiereiland Noord-Holland Midden. 110-111: all courtesy Corpus 'journey through the human body'. 112-113: Stefan Scheer /w/gnu-fdl-1.2; Jeroen Kransen /w/cc-by-sa-2.0; Stefan Scheer /w/gnu-fdl-1.2; Mech /w/gnu-fdl-1.2; courtesy Efteling. 115: Raymond Guusbosman /w/gnu-fdl-1.2. 117: F. Lamiot, /w/gnu-fdl-1.2; courtesy Het Nationale Park De Hoge Veluwe; Willemo /w/gnu-fdl-1.2; Onderwijsgek /w/cc-by-sa-2.5; /w/gnu-fdl-1.2. 118-119: W. Ponte, courtesy VVV Hoorn; S. Moeller /w/pd; S. Moeller /w/pd; S. Moeller /w/pd; paiting /pd/reproduction of Hendrick Corneliz's 'Gezicht op Hoorn' (1622), at the WestfriesMuseum Hoorn; 120-121: all courtesy Keukenhof. 122: /pd; Daiana Vasquez. 125: all pfm/jj. 127: all courtesy VVV Texel. 128: courtesy VVV Texel; lijjccoo /w/pd; /w/pd; pfm/jj. 131: Petra Stavast, courtesy Zuiderzee Museum; courtesy Zuiderzee Museum; Erik en Petra Hesmerg, courtesy Zuiderzee Museum; Petra Stavast, courtesy Zuiderzee Museum; courtesy Zuiderzee Museum. 139: all pfm/jj; Jordi character by Mike Hiscott/jj. 142-143: pfm/jj. **Back cover end paper:** /wc/gnu-fdl-1.2; 18dao.org Wiki /gnu-fdl-1.2; VVV Texel.

ACRONYMS: (cc-by-0.0) Creative Commons Attribution version #; **(cc-by-sa-0.0)** Creative Commons Attribution ShareAlike version #; **(gnu-fdl-0.0)** GNU Not Unix/ GNU Free Documentation License version #; **(jj)** Junior Jetsetters; **(pfm)** Pedro F. Marcelino; **(pd)** Public Domain; **(w)** Wikipedia/Wikimedia; **(wc)** Wikimedia Commons.

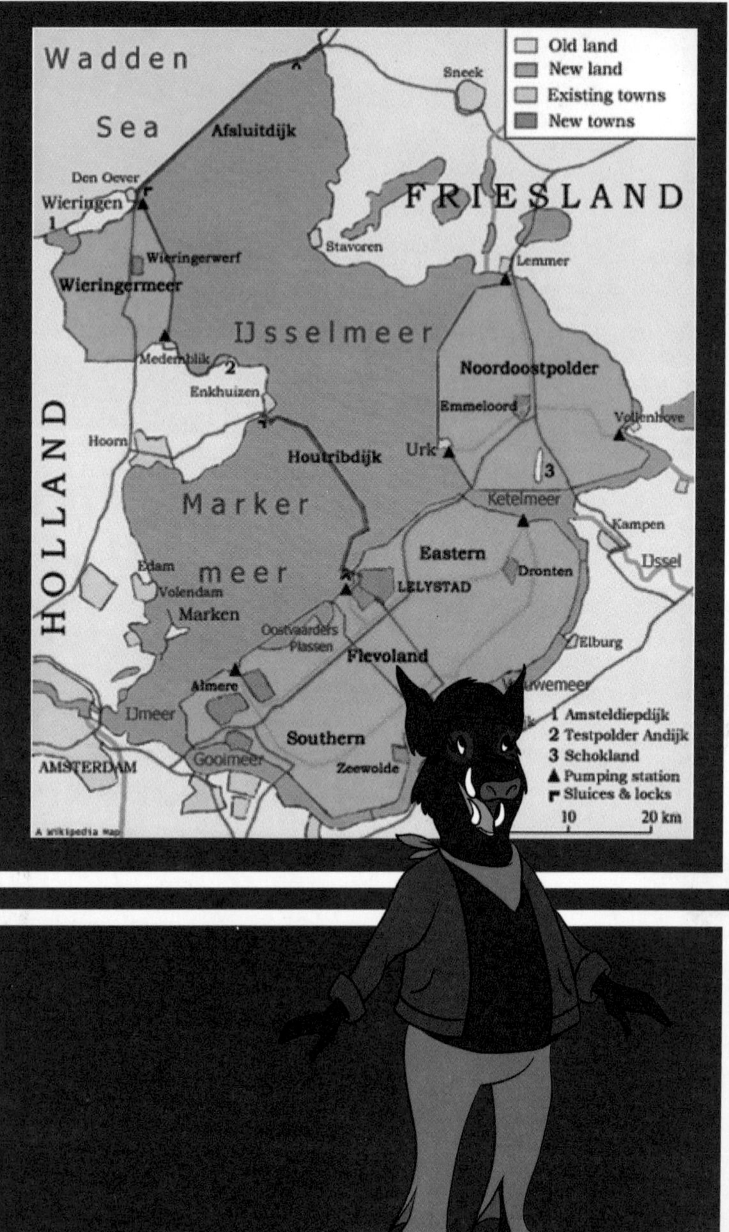

Old land
New land
Existing towns
New towns
Wadden
Sea
Afsluitdijk
Sneek
Den Oever
Wieringen
1
FRIESLAND
Stavoren
Wieringerwerf
Lemmer
Wieringermeer
IJsselmeer
Medemblik
2
Noordoostpolder
Enkhuizen
Emmeloord
HOLLAND
Hoorn
Vollenhove
Houtribdijk
Urk
3
Marker
Ketelmeer
Kampen
Eastern
Edam
meer
IJssel
Dronten
Volendam
LELYSTAD
Marken
Oostvaarders
Plassen
Elburg
Flevoland
Almere
IJmeer
1 Amsteldiepdijk
2 Testpolder Andijk
3 Schokland
Pumping station
Sluices & locks
Southern
AMSTERDAM
Gooimeer
Zeewolde
10
20 km
A wikipedia map